BUILDING ON TRADITION

THE WORK OF CURTIS & WINDHAM ARCHITECTS

BUILDING ON TRADITION

THE WORK OF CURTIS & WINDHAM ARCHITECTS

WRITTEN BY LUCY McEACHARN CURTIS

INTRODUCTION BY MARK ALAN HEWITT

FOREWORD BY MILES REDD

To our staff . . .

Though Curtis & Windham began as a two-man operation, this cloistered existence was, quite thankfully, short-lived. We quickly grew to rely upon the efforts of a talented group of individuals, the ranks of which have changed gradually over the past thirty-four years. This book represents the efforts of this whole—individuals coalescing into a firm and working to achieve a common goal. Those select few people who now hold positions of leadership within the firm are absolutely essential to the success of Curtis & Windham Architects. As such, we wish to acknowledge our associate principals and our directors, without whom we could not hope to function:

Ruben Mijares
Danny Ostendorf

Todd Beckendorff
Mark Ofield
Micaela Telleria

CONTENTS

FOREWORD BY MILES REDD
6

INTRODUCTION BY MARK ALAN HEWITT
9

PROJECTS

I. PIPING ROCK HOUSE
22

II. MEADOW LAKE HOUSE
38

III. LOOSCAN HOUSE
54

IV. BONNEY BRIER PUB
70

V. WICKERSHAM HOUSE
80

VI. BRIARWOOD HOUSE
94

VII. BURTON FARM
110

VIII. HOMEWOOD HOUSE
124

IX. CARISBROOKE FARM
142

X. INVERNESS HOUSE
156

XI. WALLISVILLE FARM
176

XII. PINE VALLEY HOUSE
188

XIII. DEL MONTE HOUSE
202

XIV. AUSTIN HOUSE
214

XV. CALIFORNIA HOUSE
226

XVI. GOOD THYME FARM
238

XVII. BRANARD HOUSE
256

XVIII. INWOOD HOUSE
270

XIX. REBA HOUSE
284

ACKNOWLEDGMENTS
302

PHOTOGRAPHY CREDITS
304

FOREWORD

Bill and Russell have been great friends and colleagues since we first met at a dinner for the Classical Institute of Architecture. I was introduced to their work by another architect and mutual friend, Gil Shafer. Gil is particularly measured and honest with his compliments, so when he was especially effusive about them and their skills, my curiosity was piqued. I found myself in immediate agreement with Gil and many other peers, clients, and collaborators.

I remember my early days working in Houston, driving around the Spanish moss–strewn streets of River Oaks, where everyone has a point of view and no one is afraid to represent. There are many architectural jewels: midcentury minimalist, black-and-white Hollywood Regency, and limestone Louis XVI piles—all often just a stone's throw away from one another. Alas, such is life in the suburbs, where an acre lot is considered large. Every so often you would see an exceptionally beautiful house (a brick Georgian with perfect details comes to mind), and my resident friend, who was driving, would affirm: "Yes, that's another Curtis & Windham house." My admiration grew, because re-creating such details over such a wide range of styles and settings is not easy to do in this day and age.

My business partner, David Kaihoi, and I have had the pleasure of working on two recent projects with Bill and Russell. These collaborations could not be any more different: one, a high-style attic addition to a French-style house, and the other a Wes Anderson–inspired getaway outside Houston. Despite the almost comical dissimilarities, Curtis & Windham approached these projects with the same considered and uncomplicated perspective that makes working with their firm an absolute joy.

With so much talent and skill, you may think both Bill and Russell would be creative shut-ins, but they are quite the opposite. You have never met two such affable and easygoing gents. It should make me pea-green with envy, but they are so nice, smart, and funny that you simply can't help but adore them. The thing about Bill and Russell, which is so clearly evidenced by this book, is that they are up for anything as long as it is done with style. Houston is an amazing place, where a convergence of incredible art, worldliness, bucks, and most importantly (and I do not say this lightly) unapologetic *fun* come together to create some of the most breathtaking backdrops the world has ever seen. To be sure, the best streetscapes often feature the work of Curtis & Windham. Of course, their architecture has restraint and correctness, yet there is always a bit of the unexpected. And that is when the joy comes through, emphasizing Dorothy Draper's evergreen and ever-relevant proverb that decorating is fun! Thank you, Bill and Russell, for bringing so much integrity and beauty to this world.

——Miles Redd

INTRODUCTION

Mark Alan Hewitt

I've worked as an architect and historian for almost half a century, and I have always relished the prospect of meeting new talent and discovering work that is excellent and intellectually stimulating. When I first encountered Curtis & Windham in the 1990s, I found their projects to be fresh and inventive. But I did not expect to return to Houston three decades later to discover how much the truly extraordinary work of the firm had transformed the city and environs. To my surprise and delight I found some of the finest traditional and classical architecture of this century in places I had come to know as a professor at Rice School of Architecture during the 1980s.

Readers of this volume will see wonderful buildings both in Texas and in far-flung locations that consistently reinforce qualities of place, as the title of an earlier monograph on the firm interpreted their architecture. Their work represents the most consistently superb design I have seen in decades, rendered persuasively in a wide variety of styles and scales. This achievement is all the more impressive when one appreciates the monumental challenges that have faced architects and builders during the past half-century.

Practicing architecture became increasingly difficult after the recessions of the early 1980s and mid-1990s, as fees and profits remained stagnant. As firms cut staff, thousands of well-trained designers left the field, leaving fewer in leadership positions as the century drew to a close. Disturbingly, many front-rank architecture schools became mired in political skirmishes between postmodernists and deconstructivists, weakening their design curricula and failing to train competent professionals. The economic turmoil that finally resulted in the Great Recession of 2008 also brought uncertainty to the building industry. This turbulent state of affairs meant that developers built little civic architecture, cultural buildings, or thoughtful housing. The shopping mall, a locus of public activity, was soon to be challenged by internet commerce, resulting in many closings. Most cataclysmic was the fall-off in office rentals after the pandemic of 2020–23, when working from home became a popular option. As the world changed, the architectural profession failed to move with it, leading to the crisis we face today.

One of the few success stories of this era was the rise of New Urbanism and New Traditional Architecture, mainly in Europe and the United States. As the public tired of seeing dull, featureless commercial and public buildings in their cities, they turned away from the monoculture of developer buildings towards smaller-scale, community-based projects by opponents of the status quo. Prince Charles built Poundbury in the UK, while Robert Davis struck gold with the new town of Seaside on Florida's panhandle. Léon Krier, Andrés Duany, Elizabeth Plater-Zyberk, Stefanos Polyzoides, and Peter Calthorpe led a vanguard of urban designers who challenged sprawl and edge-city planning strategies with their visionary proposals. Moreover, talented architects such as Allan Greenberg, John Simpson, Robert Adam, and Robert A.M. Stern built beautiful, compelling new buildings that maintained regional traditions rather than insisting on "international" modernist prototypes.

This is the context that spurred young architects during the 1990s to break with suffocating modernist doctrine and embrace place-making. Most of the new traditional designers and planners remained on the East and West Coasts of the U.S., but there were exceptional talents elsewhere, such as Thomas Norman Rajkovich in Chicago; Duncan Stroik in South Bend, Indiana; and Scott Merrill in Miami. However, none of these architects surpassed Curtis & Windham in the scope or quality of their work, or their contributions to building in their home state, Texas. Bill Curtis grew up in Longview, Russell Windham in Lazbuddie in the Panhandle, and both attended state universities before venturing out of state in their early careers. Seeking exposure to traditional architecture, they received their training in cities that offered opportunities to build in those idioms. They met when both decided to settle in Houston, the capital of the energy business. After forming their partnership, both agreed that business success would be as important as artistic distinction, and that they would endeavor to enhance the places where they built with fine traditional buildings.

To understand how and why these architects have prospered and maintained high standards during a thirty-five-year practice, this essay focuses on three essential aspects of their approach to building: the locus of their business and community, the collaborative nature of their professional practice, and the importance of region, city, and place to each project they design. To begin, the reader should understand something about River Oaks, where the two architects chose to locate both their offices and their families.

Locus: River Oaks and Houston

When Bill Curtis and Russell Windham arrived in Houston, the city was undergoing a significant transformation from its first century as the center of the oil business to a metropolis of residents from all over the globe, with a more varied economy and culture. In 1992 the city was emerging from almost a decade of slow economic growth in the wake of a reshuffling of the energy industry worldwide. Though new companies like Enron would rise and fall, the city would generally prosper from emerging markets in the decades to come. Houston would continue to grow, and its immigrant population would inject a new vitality into the metro area. New wealth would merge with old, especially in enclaves like River Oaks.

A similar transformation was happening in the design sector, as older architects were selling or closing their offices following a brutal fallow period during the 1980s. Whereas commissions were plentiful from the 1950s to the 1970s, many architects struggled to prosper when oil prices fell after the Arab oil embargo. Ronald Reagan's free market economic policies loosened restrictions on energy companies, and Houston's economy rebounded once the dust had settled. There was clearly opportunity to be had in the building and design sectors, provided strategies lined up with development trends. Though office buildings and commercial development were tapped out after the 1980s, housing and institutional sectors were underbuilt in 1990.

Houston had been a leader in the development of new housing types during the late twentieth century. In the early 2000s new construction of condominium apartments in high-rise developments slowed significantly.[1] Duplexes, townhouses, and garden apartments also saw little growth in comparison to earlier decades.[2] By the 2010s the market was in decline and many large condominium buildings were fifty years old and deteriorating, with little attention from their boards. In contrast, land in the most desirable single-family enclaves began to appreciate at a dizzying rate following the millennium, no matter what the metropolitan area. In every city, there was at least one locus of wealth and social status.

River Oaks was an ideal spot in which to locate a new architectural firm, not only for its investment potential but for its storied history. That history hinges on the efforts of two siblings, children of Governor James Stephen Hogg (1851–1906), to exploit the natural beauty and water resources of Houston's ecosystem, while also enhancing their early speculative investments along Buffalo Bayou. Will Hogg (1875–1930) used political capital and shrewd legislative reforms to create the infrastructure for a garden suburb, while his sister, Ima (1882–1975), convinced her society friends to settle in the newly planned enclave of River Oaks, oriented around both a country club and a verdant landscape. Will and Michael Hogg helped to finance Country Club Estates, a development around River Oaks Country Club, in 1923. They subsequently bought out the company and expanded its landholdings to 1,100 acres along Buffalo Bayou over a period of more than twenty years. Herbert A. Kipp designed the first subdivision as a garden suburb with long, winding streets running parallel to the bayou. Later planners continued the pattern. Though lots sold slowly at first, the development became one of the most successful of its kind in the U.S.[3]

Though the Hoggs' father had fought to constrain John D. Rockefeller and Standard Oil in Texas, he eventually teamed with Joseph S. Cullinan and two other partners to start the Texas Company, eventually to become Texaco, in 1902. Not only did his family benefit from early profits, but also from the discovery of oil on their 4,000-acre Varner plantation in West Columbia, Texas, in 1918–19. Those oil profits helped to finance the River Oaks venture, and established the Hoggs in Houston society. Eventually, through her myriad philanthropic efforts, Miss Ima used their wealth to establish the Houston Symphony Orchestra, Houston Child Guidance Center, the Houston Museum of Fine Arts, and its Bayou Bend collection of fine and decorative arts.

Bayou Bend (1926), the house that she and her brothers built with architect John F. Staub, would become the social and artistic center of the River Oaks neighborhood. Located on the largest lot facing Lazy Lane, the Hogg estate was modeled on New Orleans houses that opened to the breezes from the Gulf and Lake Pontchartrain. Miss Hogg gave her architects the plan of Homewood (1803) near Baltimore as a classical precedent, but wanted the shutters, pink stucco, and iron balconies she recalled from visits to Louisiana as a child. Its five-part plan is elegantly proportioned, while the massing is quite abstract and the façades sparsely articulated with a variety of classical details.[4] Miss Ima wanted it painted pink, a color she associated with Greece and its sunbaked landscapes. The lush gardens were the work of

Ellen Shipman, Fleming and Shepard, and Ruth London. As an ensemble of buildings and landscape, it rivals any historic estate in the United States.

Equally important, Ima Hogg furnished her house with a collection of antiques and decorative art on a par with that of Henry Francis du Pont's Winterthur, in Wilmington, Delaware. A friend of the Delaware millionaire, she competed with him at auctions and antiques sales, buying American furniture, china, silver, paintings, and anything that caught her fancy. When her collection could no longer be housed at Bayou Bend, she donated it to the Houston Museum of Fine Arts, where it is a highlight of the old wing today. All of Ima Hogg's efforts contributed to the character of her home city, and especially that of River Oaks. In crucial respects she and her collections established the benchmark for style and quality in her extended neighborhood.

Another important aspect of River Oaks is its attitude toward newcomers, one that Ima and her brothers encouraged while selling properties there. Unlike Greenwich, Connecticut, or Tuxedo Park, New York, this Houston enclave has graciously welcomed any individual or family that demonstrated its distinction in business, the arts, philanthropy, or civic work. (Eventually racist and ethnic barriers, in the initial deeds, were dropped by the corporation.) Adequate wealth was necessary, but not sufficient, for full acceptance into elite society, not only here but in the city of Houston. That attitude has allowed the city to grow and prosper while others have waned in significance—it is one of the most ethnically diverse in the nation.

So when Curtis & Windham began in 1992, the locus of their activities was River Oaks, where before 1998 they built two relatively modest but architecturally distinctive residential projects: the Park Circle House and the River Oaks House and Garden Pavilion.[5] The latter was an existing 1928 house by Cameron Fairchild located prominently on River Oaks Boulevard that the firm transformed into a magnificent Colonial Revival ensemble of buildings and gardens. The former took advantage of a wedge-shaped lot on Park Circle to place a superb Georgian townhouse amid less elegant residences from various periods. Both attracted attention and led immediately to larger projects nearby. Soon they would be the most sought-after architects in this extraordinary neighborhood, and among the best the city has seen in decades.

Practice: A Marriage of Minds

When Curtis and Windham moved to Houston, both were single. Within several years each would meet a woman with excellent credentials in her profession: the accountant Vallette Graber and the landscape architect Jane Anderson. Russell had shared space with the architect William F. Stern, next door to Ms. Graber's office. They were married in 1994. Bill Curtis met Jane Anderson through connections with the Hermann Park Conservancy, as she had been sent by her employer Laurie Olin to work on the park's new master plan. They were married in 1995.

Beginning families and forming intellectual partnerships with their spouses, Bill and Russell continued the quest that they began upon moving to Houston, an intense pursuit of design excellence and scholarly inquiry in the creation of buildings and landscapes. As their workload rapidly increased, the partners assembled a team of young designers who would staff the CWA office, understanding that they would need to choose carefully if they were to foster a traditionally oriented studio culture and efficient professional organization.

Where were they to find well-trained young designers? Neither Rice nor the University of Houston was producing graduates with knowledge of historic precedents and the classical canon. Fortuitously, several American architectural schools had begun to teach classical and traditional architecture with a seriousness not seen since the 1920s, when Paul Cret taught Lou Kahn at Penn and Jean Labatut began his tenure at Princeton. The most prominent were the University of Notre Dame and the University of Miami.

Neither was considered a front-rank school at the time, but they had visionary deans who could assemble talented faculty to build their programs in Thomas Gordon Smith and Elizabeth Plater-Zyberk, respectively. Smith convinced Rev. Theodore Hesburgh (1917–2015), the visionary president of Catholic Notre Dame, to expand its programs in Rome and reorient the school in the direction of classical architecture and urban design. A scholar-architect, Smith studied the classical tradition and brought it into his own work as early as the 1980s, fighting the hegemony of modernism in the arts. Plater-Zyberk joined with her husband, Andrés Duany, to establish the Charter of the New Urbanism and design its most famous initial town, Seaside, Florida. That achievement led to her becoming one of the first women to head an architecture school in the U.S. Her emphasis on urban and suburban planning at Miami attracted both Vincent Scully and Léon Krier to the school, as well as talented students from throughout the Southeast.

Graduates of both programs caught the attention of a new generation of classical and traditional architects both in the U.S. and abroad. When the Prince of Wales Foundation began teaching classical architecture in London under Krier's direction, students from Notre Dame and Miami were among its first graduates. They began to work with architects such as Allan Greenberg, John Blatteau, Quinlan Terry, and John Simpson, learning from emerging masters how to assemble a truly convincing classical design. Many became members of CNU, the organization established to promote traditional urbanism in America. In addition, disgruntled students from other programs became adherents to a new form of traditional architecture suited to the twenty-first century. Some are now teaching in the King's Foundation School of Traditional Arts in London.[6] Others are leading traditional architecture and planning firms.

Many talented graduates of these schools (and others) found their way to Curtis & Windham over the decades. Bill Curtis emphasizes the way in which their office fosters deep thinking and design exploration among its team of architects, landscape designers, and interior architects. It isn't enough that a staff member gets a good education or learns how to draw the classical orders. Every new hire has a period in which to learn to think in a manner appropriate to a traditional design practice. Unlike the employees in most firms, architects and designers at Curtis & Windham are required to think holistically, while also focusing on accurate and appropriate detail. The logic behind traditional architectural ornament and the corresponding integration of scale and proportion is complex, and its history requires intense study, something that few young architects understand. After about six months at the firm, all architectural staff are on the same wavelength about how a project is conceived, developed, and brought to fruition. They begin to imbibe the same habits of mind as their peers and superiors. Eventually they begin to behave as one organism, as a social network, as a team.

I have studied and written about the neuroscience of design, and how "modes of conception" bind schools of architects and artists together over time. It is not too far-fetched to suggest that a superb traditional firm—of any type—might have such a well-oiled practice that extremely high-quality results can be expected in their chosen endeavors.[7] My observation of the Curtis & Windham office indicated just this kind of coordinated environment and commitment to excellence. As young minds matured, they acquired the modes of conception required to function in this special office. A visit to the design studio confirmed my initial analysis—all the architects, landscape architects, and interior designers were fully coordinated and aware of the process required to produce high-quality work.

When I asked Bill about how the office could function so well with a staff of about thirty, he pointed to the fact that he and Russell maintained a daily practice of visiting the desks of all key designers, providing "crits" like the ones they had received from professors in school. "Both of us continue to draw and design with hand sketches, and ask our staff to do the same, to touch paper regularly," he said. Curtis continues to paint as a talented watercolorist, while Windham travels extensively and has served both as an ICAA board member and chairman for many years. In addition, Bill stressed that he and his partner agreed to share one office from the first days of their partnership, not to retreat to separate corners of a large suite. "We see each other when we arrive each morning and when we leave at night," he emphasized. Close and effective communication are essential in any partnership, whether a marriage or a business relationship.[8]

When I spoke at length with the firm's two associate principals, Danny Ostendorf and Ruben Mijares, I learned much about the process that guides all staff in working on a project over the course of its development. Danny emphasized that every incoming client is presented with a synopsis of this process before engaging the firm. From preprogramming and site analysis to interior design development, the work product is similar to that specified in standard contracts from the American Institute of Architects (AIA), but more detailed and specific in each phase. In this way, owners are brought into the process, and share in its eventual success, over time. With every member of the team engaged from day one, few projects are left on the drawing board. This record of built work is unusual for any major firm and demonstrates the soundness of Curtis & Windham's initial business plan.

Communication with clients who have varied life experiences is a challenge for any architect. By using drawings and charts based on previous projects, the staff can get new clients on track more quickly than with a purely verbal interchange. Leaving the owners with a brief "user's manual" has proven to be a secret to "controlling expectations," as the expression goes. Though the partners pointed to a few missteps and strained relationships, the number was small compared to most medium-sized firms. Danny and Ruben also stressed the need for regular meetings and remote conferences on their part, to keep owners connected to the ongoing phases of each project. They understand their roles as intermediaries between the partners and their clients.

The superb quality of nearly every individual building in the firm's portfolio is a testament to this high standard, but there is more to the essential appropriateness and beauty of their houses, gardens, and institutional projects than formulaic design procedures. All of these buildings have a distinct relationship to the places they inhabit, contributing to its character over many years. That close correspondence of building and site is another telltale sign of the firm's success. The projects in this volume each demonstrate how a close reading of the site informs the design of exterior and interior elements.

fig. 1. Good Thyme Farm

fig. 2. Carisbrooke Farm

Places: From Farm to Folly

Nothing in the portfolio of Curtis & Windham is out of tune with its neighborhood, town, or region. Every building fits its purpose, contributes to the quality of its environment, and enhances its community. Though of varying styles and in diverse locations, each work presents a coherent attitude toward place, fitting its location like a glove. That can hardly be said of the most prominent architects and planners in Houston or the U.S., no matter what their status in the profession. Often contemporary buildings are jarringly out of tune with their surroundings, and trumpet their formal and stylistic dissonance as a virtue.

To understand how CWA designs with place-making in mind, one might begin with a recent project in the town of Bellville, an hour from Houston. This small courthouse town has grown due to an influx of Houstonians wanting weekend retreats with the rustic feel of historic Texas farms—not ranches, but farms. Bill Curtis, who has owned one such farm for over two decades, described the landscape around Bellville as hilly, but not as rugged as the picturesque Hill Country in West Texas. Texas Germans began farming the area north and east of San Antonio during the early nineteenth century. Food production for the restaurant trade flourishes in this region, supplying eateries in all the surrounding cities.

The clients for Good Thyme Farm were deeply connected to the world of food, and though they first acquired the farm as a retreat for their young family, they quickly evolved the property into a system of support for their interest in farm-to-table restaurants in Houston. On approaching their house near Bellville, one finds a newly refurbished and expanded compound at the center of a rustic farm, where food is grown, chefs are educated, and strong culinary relationships are forged.

As the architects write, "to generate a richer experience for a structure such as this, we deferred primarily to the story of the landscape." Retaining the modest farmhouse at the center of a farm and garden complex, the design team reoriented the ensemble around a new block-with-dependencies house, with each wing addressing a particular space on the cardinal axes of the property. Most of the farm structures were restored or adapted to serve the farm-to-table business on a year-round basis. The new "farmscape" is also a kind of academic quadrangle, as incubating fresh culinary ideas is also part of the program. New structures include a trailer pad, tennis courts, farm buildings, vegetable and herb gardens, and animal pens for goats, chickens, and sheep. Longhorn cattle graze happily on surrounding pastures. The agricultural landscape is entirely in keeping with historical examples throughout the region, but with a slightly whimsical and playful tinge.

That character extends to the interiors of the new house. Miles Redd and David Kaihoi, New York decorators, were friends of the owners and architects, and provided extraordinary design ideas for every room. The main living room is a circus of artifacts and useful items that offer comfort and visual delight at every turn. The kitchen is a play space for cooks, a laboratory for catering experiments, and it opens to an informal dining space that could be in a roadside café. Each bedroom/bathroom suite has a theme and zingy color scheme. The house feels like an entertainment wonderland within a cozy country inn.

Though Curtis & Windham's first book, *A Vision of Place*, contains several splendid ranches and rustic country houses, it does not feature these types of farmsteads and weekend retreats. Carisbrooke Farm, Wallisville Farm and Burton Farm have many of the characteristics of the Bellville project, including its palette of mainly wood materials and subtle classical references. Bill Curtis explained that the clientele for these more recent retreats was River Oaks–based, but that they were often content to eschew some of the expectations of city houses in favor of a vernacular rusticity that would better suit their rural locales. Acutely attuned to creating experiences associated with country places and their history, the architects directed their research and design focus to these contexts. Their approach was no less scholarly but demanded a much greater understanding of rural history, agricultural practices, and a site's relationship to the surrounding landscape.

fig. 3. Pine Valley House

fig. 4. Piping Rock House

The economic and real estate situation also shifted during the recent decades, offering fewer large lots for development and more opportunities for sensitive additions and renovations in various areas of River Oaks. So although some larger house commissions were forthcoming, the firm designed several delightful smaller houses that are featured in this volume. The Pine Valley House is located across the street from Russell Windham's own in River Oaks. As he explained, the clients wanted to maintain the character of the neighborhood and thus designed a "modest and well-mannered" suburban villa with a fountain in the rear yard and an intimate porch opening to the main rooms. The owners wanted to downsize after their children were launched, and they love the new house. There is an elegant kitchen in the center of the main wing that serves as the organizing locus and has views of all the main rooms and garden. Precedents for the brick-and-wood exterior include Shingle style, Queen Anne, and Arts & Crafts houses on both sides of the Atlantic.

A similar essay in English Arts & Crafts design is the unusual two-lot house with a main façade on Inverness. "The primary axis of the joined properties is only revealed once a visitor has progressed past the front gate, which is stationed at the back of the public auto court," the architects explained. What would have been a rear garden and courtyard becomes the main entrance façade, with the Inverness front presenting a symmetrical Surrey country house to those passing by. The architects succeeded in replicating the kind of brick and stucco walls that are common in Lutyens houses in the south of England.

The interiors also maintain the English theme with an open living room adjoining the stair hall, with its Lutyens-inspired metal balustrade. The formal dining room faces a large bar that opens to one of the main circulation axes. Most rooms have garden views, including a large library and office. There is an adjoining pool house that serves a relatively small plunge pool. Like so many of their house and garden plans, this ensemble is a jigsaw puzzle of intriguing spaces that are interlocked masterfully.

The lots in River Oaks vary in size from one sector to another, and the armatures that they create shift in equal measure from block to block. In the district in which we find the Wickersham House, small gardens were added to knit themselves into the flow of the dwelling. The plan forms a *Z* to allow each wing a view of the exterior, with low walls defining intimate gardens. Auto access is from the side street so there is no driveway to interrupt the green space of the house. A beautiful multi-arched brick doorway gives access to a hall and views of the living room, elegantly decorated by Wolf Holden Design Studio of Houston. The stair hall is a nod to Lutyens's brilliant Homewood, with white balusters leading to a well-lit second-floor hall. Houston's favorite architect, John Staub, also used this house as an inspiration for some of his Houston residences, something noted by the architects. This room organizes the bedrooms and continues the Arts & Crafts theme of the exterior. There are less-formal rooms at the rear of the property, each surrounded by lush gardens. The wife's painting studio is a surprise accessed by the clever back stair, also with painted balusters in the "negative" shape of the front stair.

These brilliant house/garden plans are indicative of Curtis & Windham's holistic approach to site design. Every lot has its own shape, orientation, and context. Thus, whether the house is large or small, Georgian or Tudor, the strategies are similar when the goal is to provide a sense of place, comfort, and elegance. This is particularly true of two spectacular houses for collectors: the Piping Rock House and the Meadow Lake House.

The latter was designed around a collection of American Regency furniture passed from mother to daughter. A classical, white brick and stucco villa was the appropriate type for the site. It proved to be an ideal formal armature for arranging formal rooms around a semicircular stair hall. Exterior features include an elegant Federal doorway, several bow windows, and pilasters with fluted capitals. The formal rooms were each designed to feature key pieces of furniture: the hall opposite the stair focuses on an elaborately carved sofa and two equally elegant gilt sconces. The superb dining room has a niche for a large serving table and an Ionic screen to flank the antique piano. There is even a John Soane–inspired breakfast room to complement the paneled kitchen.

The Regency villas of John Nash are distant cousins of the Piping Rock House, located on a prominent corner lot. A hint of the owner's elegant taste greets visitors at the front door, with its Greek key pattern in black and white opening onto a curving staircase that is dramatically lit by a distant skylight. The three-bay main block is flanked on the left by a pergola wing, while the opposite side has no symmetrical wing. This makes room for a bowing stair hall that faces a broad lawn. Indeed, semicircular windows and projections are a theme on each main façade.

fig. 5. Del Monte House

fig. 6. Homewood House

The architects call this an Italian *piano nobile*–inspired house since all its public and formal rooms are on the second floor. The wall opposite the monumental stair is rustic, indicating that private rooms like bedrooms and mudrooms are located beyond. Indeed the upstairs rooms are all memorable, with a large formal *salle* greeting visitors first. The dining room facing the rear is relatively small, but superbly furnished with antiques. Perhaps the most impressive room is the owner's private library, in green and white. Craftsmanship in the millwork, plaster cornices, floors, and hardware is uniformly superb, indicative of the architects' broad reach into the trades. The glass and gilt balusters of the stair are remarkable.

Curtis & Windham are known in Houston for their allegiance to clients' needs and requirements, no matter what the scale of each project. As they like to say, "we serve our clients as designers, advisors, and professionals." When additions or renovations to an existing house are warranted, they devote the same care to this work as to larger commissions. This was the case in both the Del Monte House and the Homewood House, each with its own challenges and opportunities.

When a New York couple with Texas roots bought a first-generation French Provincial manor adjacent to River Oaks Boulevard and near the country club, the architects recognized that its prominent site required special treatment. A vacant corner lot was part of the property, providing space for new rooms and garden features. Their young children would have spaces to play in the yard without attracting the attention of neighbors. By creating a separate entrance "for partygoers" on the Boulevard, screened by a hedge, the architects could leave the handsome formal doorway alone and hide a new garage as well. They also added a charming pool cabana in the form of a covered porch. Houston decorator Randy Powers spiced up the interiors with subtle gray and brown color schemes. The elegant kitchen and adjoining family room are standouts in the new/old house.

Hugo Neuhaus was one of Houston's pioneering Miesian architects working in the 1950s and '60s on a variety of classic houses.[9] His own residence (1950), on Lazy Lane, came up for sale recently, and though some architects might have found such a landmark modernist renovation intimidating, Bill and Russell took the challenge in stride. The clients were "fearless" in changing the décor in major rooms, pushing the designers to stretch their imaginations. Curtis & Windham also added new spaces for increased leisure activities, without compromising the order of the site: a spa and Roman-style caldarium and tepidarium replaced an existing guest house; so a distant outdoor garden structure was replaced by a joint office and guesthouse, fulfilling a similar role.

The Cambridge, Massachusetts, landscape firm Reed Hilderbrand designed the dramatic new gardens and paths linking new buildings to old, giving the site a coherence that had vanished with preceding landscape designs. The clients already had a fine collection of contemporary art from many of today's noted artists to hang on large walls throughout the residence, and their decorators had a field day matching furniture and lighting around each painting or sculpture. Even the new powder room became an art showcase.

fig. 7. Branard House

fig. 8. Bonney Brier Pub

Having a bit of fun with these kinds of commissions has kept the partners and staff loose enough to indulge in some whimsical, small-scale building projects that might almost be called "follies" in the English sense. To wit, when Bill and Jane Curtis relocated from their family-sized house in River Oaks they decided to buy a small, thin lot in the museum district for their "empty nester" downsizing project. The Branard House was quite literally built around a huge live oak tree whose low-hanging branches extend over fifty-five feet from the trunk, making it imperative that foundations and walls were well clear of its root system. An L-shaped plan proved ideal for both function and style as the couple laid out their ideal bungalow, oriented toward the Menil Collection quadrant just north of the site.

Though the exterior is quite modest, all the major rooms are full of clever conceits based on historical precedents. The large library/family room has a massive wall of books flanked by floor-to-ceiling windows framing a patio almost entirely filled with tree branches. A winding stair leads to the spacious upper landing, featuring a mural-sized Giambattista Nolli map of Rome. Bedrooms and baths are located at either end of this airy room, each both comfortable and artful as decorated by frequent collaborators Ann Wolf and Ashley Holden, of Wolf Holden Design Studio. Bill parried comments about the "folly" of buying such a difficult site by showing ingenuity and flexibility in equal measure in the final design.

When a valued client asked the firm for an enhancement to their home, a previous Curtis & Windham project facing a championship golf course, the architects might well have taken offense. After all, the 2005 Bonney Brier House had a pool room and study as part of its sprawling California ranch layout and the family seemed happy with their country residence. To their surprise, the architects were shown photographs of the Jigger Inn, a small pub near the famed St. Andrews Old Course in Scotland, which our clients had come to know both as avid golfers and parents of students at the nearby university. They spent happy hours there, sipping Scotch, talking about British Open tournaments with their friends, and catching up with their children. Would their architects in Houston be willing to create a similar, or even identical, pub adjacent to their home but also visible from the golf course?

This unusual design commission proved to be not only enjoyable but also creatively stimulating, as most commissions are not undertaken solely for fun and deepening social relationships. Though their Bonney Brier Pub would be quite small by comparison to the original, it would not lack authentic heirlooms, décor, and even English libations "imported" from the source. In a single room the architects created a rich and dramatic setting evocative of its Scottish inspiration.

The joyful appreciation of history that attends nearly every Curtis & Windham design is epitomized in this miniature ale house, infusing every inch of its interior with wit and humor. The small bar is beautifully detailed to evoke examples of the British Isles, and seating areas adjacent are also rife with the flavor of cozy nooks in Ireland and Scotland's famed pub interiors. Red, green, and blue are the theme colors, enlivened by tartan fabric and wood accents. The owner spent hours curating each souvenir of St. Andrews and choosing rare ales and Scotches for the bar. Her work has paid off, as members of the country club have become "regulars" at their establishment. Often they enter the pub in the evening to find "tips" in the jar at the bar and signatures in the guest book, even from strangers who have stopped by before concluding their round.

British architecture has for centuries reveled in the "folly" of garden buildings and humorous temples dedicated to the pleasures of nature and her mythic creatures. It is fitting that two architects steeped in these design traditions should be drawn to creating their own follies, whether in a garden setting or on a golf course. On my visit to the Bonney Brier, I found myself back in Scotland, if only for a moment, as perhaps many an English peer has imagined himself in Rome or Athens while seated in his belvedere overlooking meadows and glades. Read *Brideshead Revisited* and you will understand what I mean. There is an English sensibility for design that requires literacy in the classics, and a deep learning that comes with experiencing great architecture over a lifetime.

That kind of literacy is rare among American architects, and hardly common today among the best designers in the world. Bill Curtis and Russell Windham have it. Practicing in Texas, but looking for inspiration around the world, gave them the opportunity to prove that talent and commitment to excellence are not confined to the so-called art centers in Europe or the Eastern U.S. Walking in the footsteps of Ralph Adams Cram, John Staub, William Ward Watkin, and Birdsall Briscoe, they fit the mold of those "academic" eclecticists of the old school. Winning the prestigious Arthur Ross Award for architecture in 1999 proved that they would become leaders in the profession. They continue to surprise the architecture world with their superb design and craftsmanship, and this book won't be the last to document their achievements. You'll find much to enjoy in the pages that follow.

Notes

1. Richard Buday, "Condocide: Death of a Building Type," *Common Edge*, 5/15/23; https://commonedge.org/condocide-death-of-a-building-type/
2. For a description of new types see Mark A. Hewitt, "The Stuff of Dreams: New Suburban Housing in Houston," *CITE*, Summer, 1985, 13–15. For garden apartments, see Peter C. Papademetriou, "Magnificent Courtyards, Beautiful Fountains," *Via 4: Culture and the Social Vision*, Univ. of Pennsylvania, 1980.
3. Torrie Hardcastle, "Houston's Most Expensive Neighborhoods," *Houston Chronicle*, 9/25/15, n.p. accessed online at www.chron.com/homes/article/Houston-s-20-most-expensive-neighborhoods-5781376.php#photo-6913644.
4. For a detailed account of the house see Howard Barnstone, *The Architecture of John F. Staub* (Austin: University of Texas Press, 1977): 106–113. On Ima Hogg's life and building the estate, see David F. Warren, "Ima Hogg and Bayou Bend: A History," *Bulletin of the Museum of Fine Arts* (Houston) 12:1 (Fall 1988), 2–12. For a treatment of the house in relation to its contemporaries, see Mark Alan Hewitt, *The Architect and the American Country House: 1890–1940* (New Haven: Yale University Press: 1990), 234–237.
5. Both were published in *A Vision of Place: The Work of Curtis & Windham Architects* (College Station: Texas A&M Univ. Press, 2018), 20–23 and 38–43.
6. On the programs see: https://schooloftraditionalarts.org
7. Mark Alan Hewitt, *Draw In Order to See: A Cognitive History of Architectural Design* (San Francisco, ORO Editions: 2020).
8. See Mark Alan Hewitt, "NeoClassicism and Modern Architecture, Houston Style, or the Domestication of Mies," *CITE*, Fall 1984, 12–15.
9. Ibid.

PROJECTS

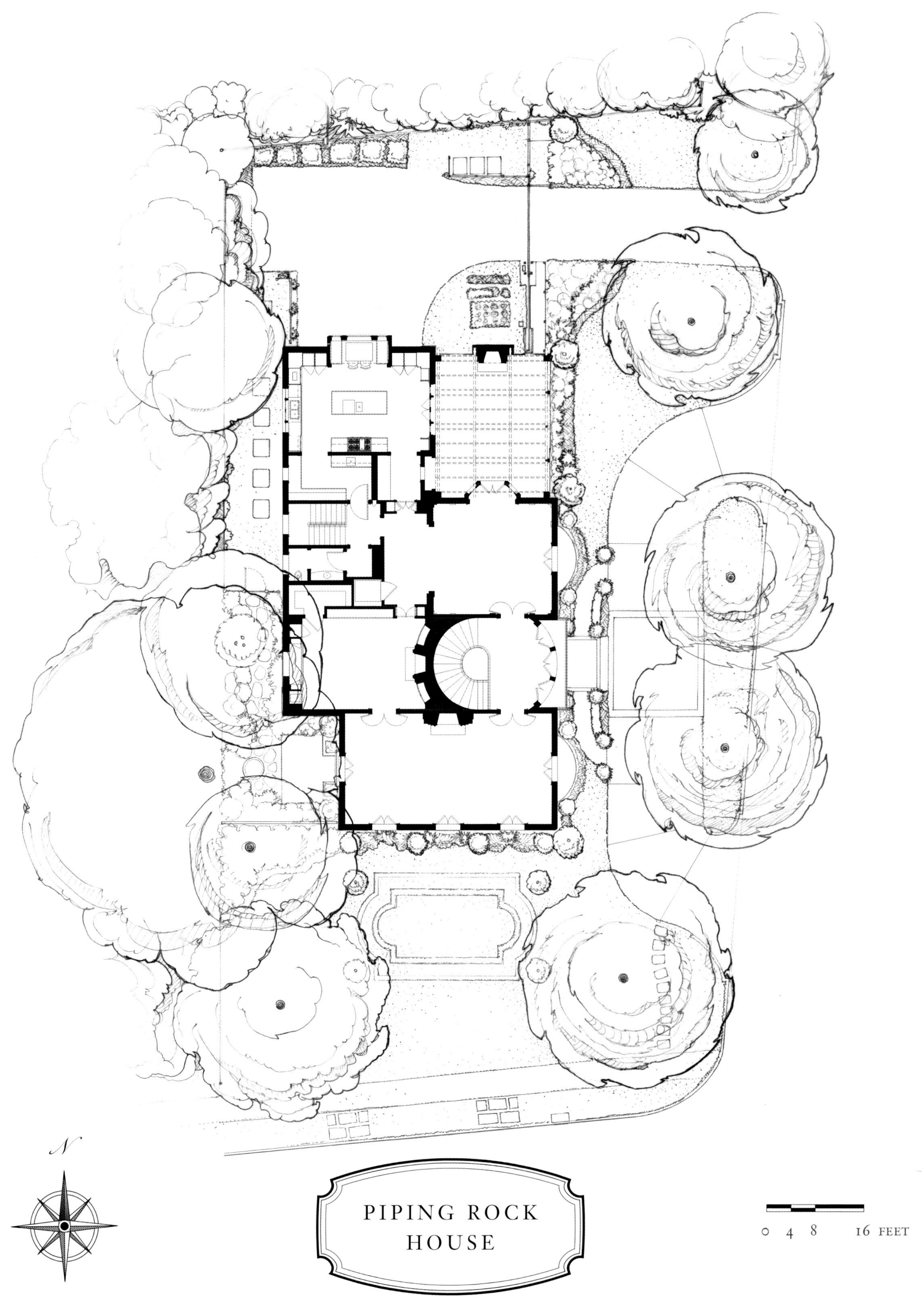
N
PIPING ROCK
HOUSE
0 4 8 16 FEET

I. PIPING ROCK HOUSE

The primary method by which this River Oaks residence diverges from the conventions of the neighborhood is hardly legible from the exterior unless you know precisely where to look. This project, on a highly visible corner lot, was designed to blend in contextually on the outside but subvert expectations on the inside. From its white-painted brick exterior to its contemporaneous mix of Art Deco flair and classical characteristics, it is quintessentially befitting of the neighborhood without bearing down too completely on any one traditional architectural style. But to step even one foot inside the front door is to confront the complete functional inversion that is a *piano nobile*, or "noble floor" in the original Italian, usually what we would consider the second story. Unlike other houses, the first floor of this home is held back from public use; all of the formal rooms, those oriented towards the entertainment of guests, are housed on the floor upstairs, with bedrooms and private spaces taking up primary residence down below.

Our client's leading suggestion to design a *piano nobile* that would neatly blend into its surroundings was a welcome challenge and one that we had long been hoping to meet. In this neighborhood of two-story houses, we consciously diverged from the primary definition of a *piano nobile*, which would typically feature in a house of at least three floors, with communal ventures on the ground floor and personal spaces up above. We carried forward the inverted characteristics of the design, restricting the building's height to better fit its context.

The front door opens onto a grand stair hall, in one of the few prototypical gestures of the plan. Even so, this rusticated interior space, with its warm gray wooden siding, signals to visitors that though they may yet be sheltered inside, the formal entry of the house stretches out above them, not directly in front. Doors branch off to the left and right, leading to the primary bedroom, office, and guest room, respectively. The staircase, adorned with echoes of the front door's Greek key motif, beckons guests onwards and upwards. Far above, a circular skylight lets an abundance of natural light into the stair hall—cool, luminous, and engaging.

Greek-inspired moldings on either side of the upstairs landing lend a robust and masculine profile to what might ordinarily be considered a liminal space. They support the landing's desire to be recognized as a threshold without entering into the dreaded territory of overembellishment. Past this point, the expansive living room occupies one entire side of the second floor. From there, circulation passes into the library, dining room, out onto the terraced balcony, and back, in an endless, intuitive flow. In the far corner of the living room, we stationed a voluminous palm tree that amplifies the eclectic nature of our interior design. Its striking height and mass draw attention to the volumetric ceilings of the second floor, a sneaky feature derived from the incorporation of several vertical feet of attic space.

We drew inspiration for the interiors from an odd mix of sources: the black and white, paneled library walls with their anomalous sections of green velvet inlay were an emulation of a library from the Château du Groussay in Montfort-l'Amaury, France, while the highly glazed dining room walls represent our interpretation of the eggplant-colored Rolls-Royce that once belonged to Queen Elizabeth II. These latter, deeply reflective surfaces provide a striking contrast to the dining room's much lighter architectural details and double as a playful conversation starter for all dinner parties held therein.

In contrast to the oftentimes elaborate interior design, our handling of the surrounding landscape was relatively subdued. On the open terrace, which is accessible from the second floor, we positioned a wooden arbor to one day provide shelter from the hot Southern sun. Flowering vines planted on three corners of the terrace will slowly crawl toward each other across the width of the framework, shading as they go. The surrounding landscape is restrained, refined, and unfailingly symmetrical, in keeping with the adjacent house's classical mannerisms. In a gesture of private intrigue, we sunk a small, recessed garden into the southern easement, which rests shallowly below the level of the surrounding lawn. This unobtrusive feature easily evades notice from passersby on the street or sidewalks, but when gazing out down from the balconies above, the contrasting gravel walkways and green shades of the plant life provide a secret point of interest for the owner and his guests.

EMBASSY RESIDENCES

International Atlas
ATLAS OF THE WORLD
NATIONAL GEOGRAPHIC ATLAS OF THE WORLD

FROM THE PRIVATE COLLECTIONS OF TEXAS
ICONS OF STYLE
VALENTINO

Great Houses of HAVANA
FALLINGWATER
VANDERBILT
ALBERT SPEER
THE WHITE HOUSE
WHITE HOUSE CHINA
AUDUBON'S AVIARY
KLIMT
Les Orientalistes
The ROYAL PALACES of SPAIN
SILVER in AMERICA
TIFFANY SILVER FLATWARE
TIFFANY PARTIES

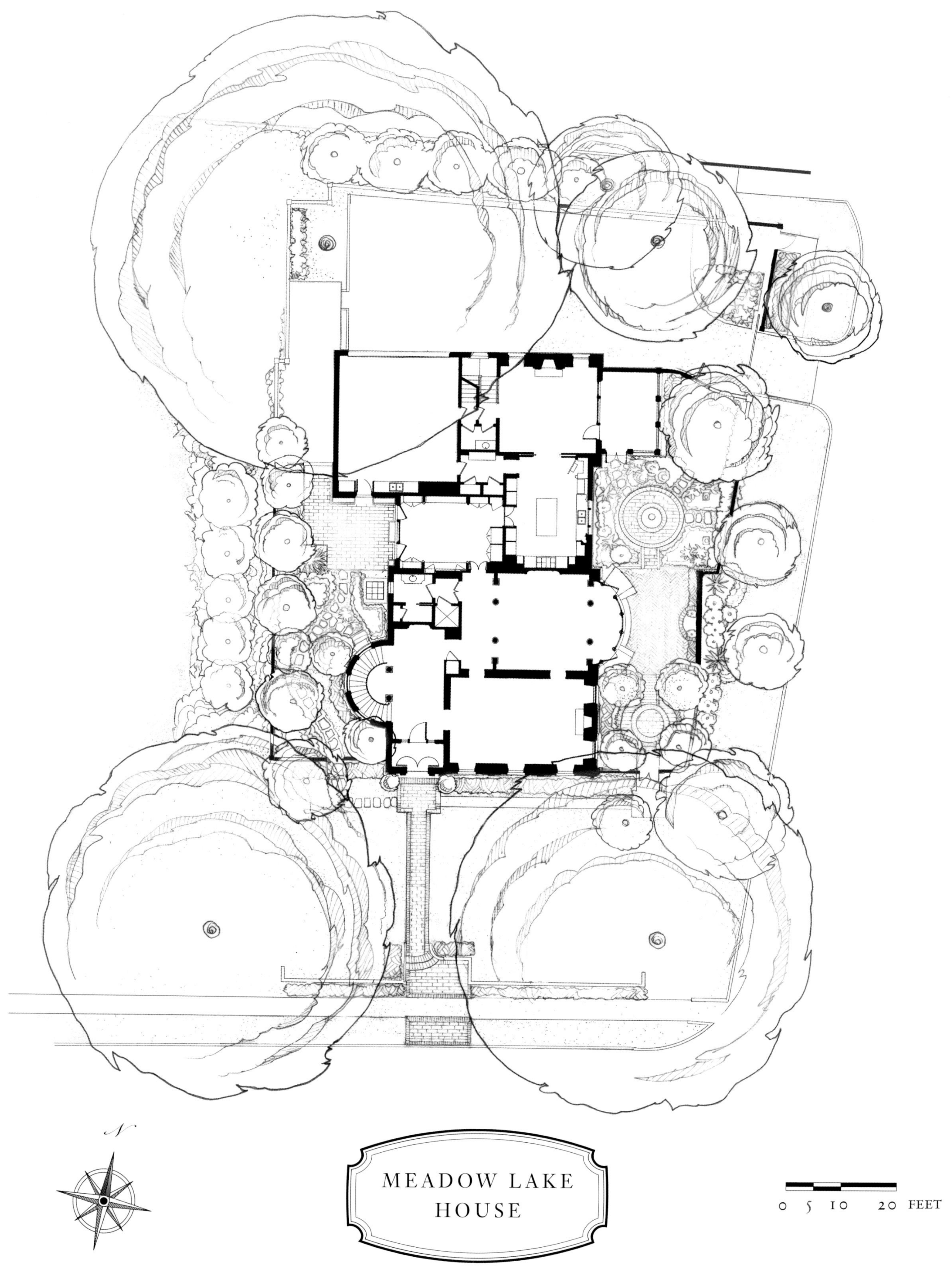
MEADOW LAKE
HOUSE
0 5 10 20 FEET
N

II. MEADOW LAKE HOUSE

Many years ago, a mother passed down her collection of American Regency furniture to her daughter, who continued to grow and care for the collection to maintain that meaningful family tradition. Eventually, the collection became substantial enough to warrant a new home, one that could specifically tailor its environment to its contents, and the daughter became our client. With the resulting house, we sought to provide a measure of formality that would sufficiently complement the display of traditional furnishings, with their dark wood and intricately carved and turned, often claw-footed legs. However, it could not be rendered so formal as to become austere, unyielding to the comforts of the lives lived inside its walls.

In searching for a precedent coincident with the heritage of the home's contents, we looked to the American Federal and Regency periods, whose restrained, carefully proportionate characteristics would allow our building to coexist affably with the surrounding houses without sacrificing its principled character. In keeping with these styles, the mass of the building is of a simple geometry with a classically rendered, symmetrical façade. Evenly spaced windows rest in recessed arches, separated on either axis by pilasters and a thin belt course, attenuated and detailed in a manner coincident with the character of the English Regency period. The entryway is further dignified through the institution of a full Ionic order. Inside, we composed a series of canonical rooms that would respect the formal qualities of the furniture and provide a layer of architectural depth without sacrificing comfort.

We articulated the front of the white brick house above its other visible sides with an additional, articulated layer of stucco known as parging. Parging, a pre–Industrial Revolution method of waterproofing low-fired brick, had been rendered functionally obsolete by the progression of quality building materials, but the traditional aesthetic value it holds presented yet another opportunity for distinction. This distinguished exterior treatment increases the formality of the house and lends a period-appropriate interest to its street-facing façade. Consequently, this choice aligns with the constraints imposed by the neighboring houses, midblock properties whose contributions to the neighborhood's fabric hinge entirely on the aesthetic characteristics of their front façades.

Inside, a double-cubed entry hall greets visitors with an axial view that draws focus down the full length of the room. On the left side of this hall, we grounded a gestural, winding staircase in a lofty, semicircular vestibule that projects off the side of the house's symmetrical core. A notable source of inspiration for this space came from the great body of Robert Adam's neoclassical work. Like Adam, we employed Doric columns, decorative plaster moldings, direct focal points, and a crosswork of ceiling beams whose geometrical lines echo the pattern of the two-toned tiled floor below.

From there, visitors proceed into the living room through a door on the right side of the entry hall, where five large, lavishly curtained windows throw bright Southern light onto the interior. French tier-on-tier shutters lend a measure of privacy to the street-facing room and protect the delicate interior furnishings from the persistent sunlight. Overall, sparse architectural details work to strike a careful balance between the antique furniture, silk curtains, and delicately patterned rug.

Two doorways link the living room to the dining room and facilitate the well-ordered flow of movement from one formal space to another. Inside the dining room, two pairs of Ionic columns establish a perfectly square floor plan, the natural geometrical complement to a circular table. One pair of these columns frames a grand piano that sits in the extra floor space created by a curvilinear bay window, while the other pair distinguishes an open corridor that skirts along the side of the dining room and leads farther into the house. The breakfast room also contains a perfect square, though it differs in style through the inclusion of a paper-vaulted ceiling. The windows at the far end of this room open out onto a border of gardens, which wrap around the open sides of the house.

Though undoubtedly highly principled, the architecture of this house is not restrictive; it is the unifying factor that runs throughout the home, organizing and balancing as it goes. Formal axes not only direct the flow of movement from room to room, but constantly shift focus outward toward the light, a reminder that no house can rely on architecture alone to sustain a meaningful presence within its environment.

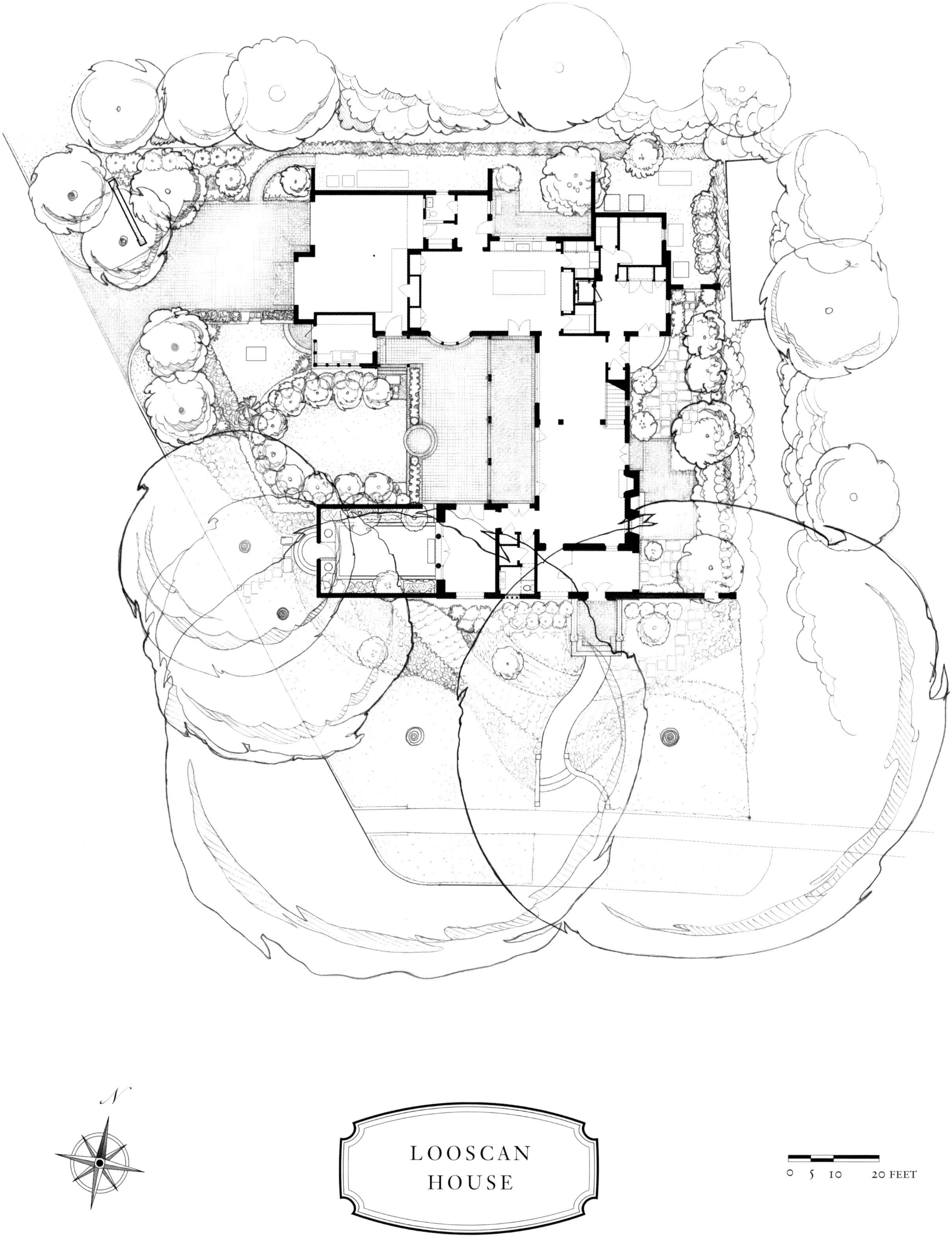

N

LOOSCAN
HOUSE

0 5 10 20 FEET

III. LOOSCAN HOUSE

This house stands on a corner lot, shielded by a line of mature, twisting oak trees, and steeped on three sides in strong Texas sunlight. Red-tiled roofs and bright stucco walls readily absorb and diffuse this heat, while a series of steel windows and doors provides easy access from the shady interiors to the welcoming gardens that wrap around the perimeter of the house. Simple forms work in conjunction with the effects of sun and shade to marry the house with its surroundings, aided by a minimal palette of color and materials. In the first of many interactions between house and lot, the building's white exterior provides an ideal background for the aforementioned trees, which cast cool gray dappled shadows across the entrance.

From the onset of this project, our clients' vision of a pure, almost vernacular form of architectural expression sent us down a path of design in which solidity and permanence are structural components, and aesthetics are primarily functional. To achieve these goals, we relied on the behavioral characteristics of our chosen materials to dictate the clarity of our response. Plaster, for one, is essentially mud. It is fluid and plastic, and though it is capable of holding on to a shape as it dries, it will not bear complex details when handled outside a mold. We replicated the simple, sculptural, elegant, historic details for which plaster and stucco are well suited throughout the house. They are visible where the mantel of the fireplace in the principal bedroom flows upward to join smoothly with the wall's surface, or outside, where the descending line of the chimney meets with the vertical plane of the house. This lack of overt embellishment trains the eye to pick up moments of intrigue it might otherwise overlook, such as the swirling black shadows cast by iron window latches onto natural-toned walls or the knots and whorls of the antique wood ceiling panels. These carefully curated materials are plainly beautiful and do not seek to accomplish any manner of detail work for which they are unsuited. They stand in for the visual intrigue of more typically decorative elements while retaining and reinforcing the house's well-built, solid, and substantial character.

In keeping with this character, the plaster walls are thickly rendered; a triple layer of material coats each surface. The practical effect of this thickness is distinctive, cool, and solidly mannered. Even so, the house does not exist as a completely closed form. A sizable series of steel windows and doors opens up the lines of sight and facilitate movement between the interior and exterior. Several distinct areas of landscape design encourage a gradual transition from the house to the garden and back again.

With this transition, we have followed in the footsteps of a long line of architects who have found that Houston's annual weather patterns adapt easily to the style of Mediterranean-inspired architecture, whose interconnected plans encourage a life lived equally in and out of doors. Our temperate winters allow for the cultivation of gardens year-round, which more than makes up for the affliction of summer. In respect of this relationship, we played with the massing of the house to create moments of interaction between the structure of the house and our landscape design. On the building's west face, where the living and dining spaces open onto a partially covered terrace, the mass of the house steps out on either side to envelop the outlying courtyard gardens within its cool, sturdy arms. A combination of stucco walls and developing hedges provide a bit of privacy from the motion of the street, particularly around the outlying planting beds, but they are not so tall as to completely sequester our clients out of sight of the neighborhood. For all of its sturdiness and certainty of form, the house maintains a sense of connectivity that travels throughout the property, jumping from wall to wall, from terrace to balcony, from tree to tile, from shadowy corner to bright swath of Southern sunlight.

E.K

AMERICAN CITIES
ICONIC

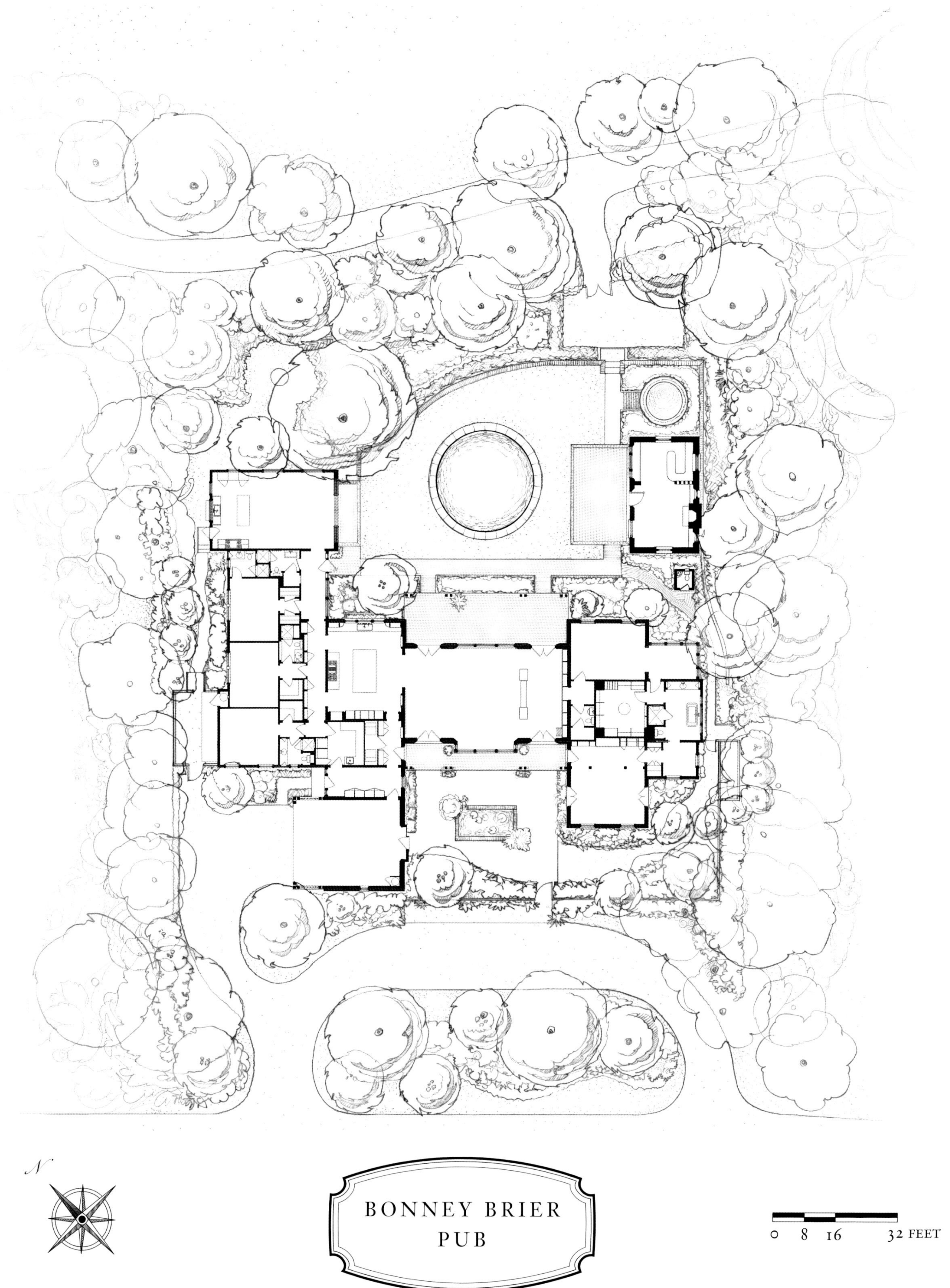
N
BONNEY BRIER
PUB
0 8 16 32 FEET

IV. BONNEY BRIER PUB

Our clients, frequent fliers of the firm, came to us with the novel idea to design a freestanding pub in their backyard, one that could be directly accessed from the adjacent fairway of Houston's Champions Golf Club. This small addition to their property engages the course casually, augmenting the family's social existence on the slice side of the fairway, where the adjacent houses are exposed to a near-constant barrage of errant golf balls. A string of wayfaring golfers following the unpredictable path of these objects now find themselves stalling their carts at the foot of this pub, brimming with curiosity and suddenly hounded by thirst. Our clients were conscious of the attention they might garner through the creation of such a conspicuous attraction. Their jovial attitude on the matter is best demonstrated by the inclusion of the low iron gate in the boundary fence of their property, adorned with a custom sign that reads, in a lighthearted replication of that of the St. Andrews Golf Club, "*Private - Members Only* / The Slice Side, est. 2022."

The pub itself is a joyful yet deferential distillation of one of the family's favorite UK pubs, the Jigger Inn in St. Andrews, Scotland. That original is a repurposed stationmaster's lodge dating back to the 1850s, and rests precariously on the edge of the famed seventeenth hole of the Old Course. The Inn was too large to be reproduced in its entirety, so we set about concentrating its essence and form into a smaller structure that would suit the property and the scale of the adjacent house. The Bonney Brier Pub consists of a small outdoor beer garden and a one-room building, containing within its walls several episodic moments reminiscent of the original pub's more spacious furnishings. This organization allows patrons to seek the comfort of the seating area of their choosing, be it a barstool, stuffed armchair, banquette, or poker table.

In designing the pub, we were intent on maintaining the aesthetic language of both the Scottish source material and the original Bonney Brier house, which we had designed and built several years earlier. The black door and window frames speak to the former purpose, while the whitewashed brick façade and the exposed rafters supporting a wood-shingled roof address the latter. In this process of developing authenticity, the owners provided much-needed first-person knowledge of the Jigger Inn and spent invaluable amounts of time curating the decorative objects and furnishings that would most accurately represent their memory of that place. On the interior, the new pub brims with color, pattern, and texture. It borrows the bold color scheme of the Jigger Inn, but the paned windows and warm light fixtures, combined with the medium-toned wooden interior details, brighten up the space considerably. The decor is composed of original paraphernalia from St. Andrews, situationally appropriate family heirlooms, and vintage pieces, none seeming gratuitous or out of place. Each piece carries an air of thoughtful authenticity, from the tartans to the bespoke barware, poker chips to the golf trophies. The bar's cache of genuine Scottish liquor, discreetly smuggled out of the country by our clients and their family members, makes for a unique offering. When standing on the edge of the fairway, golfers can catch a glimpse of the bar through the side window of the pub, and the golden glow of whisky on the shelves is a welcoming beacon that draws in friends and family—members only, of course—through the gate.

The earnest quality of the project is, among many crowd-pleasing features, the most likely explanation for the pub's cultlike status among visitors to the golf club. The building was primarily intended for use by the client's family and friends, the private members of their social circle, but their patronage has grown as word of the pub's existence has circulated around the club and the course alike. Nowadays, the family will often enter the pub to find that some passersby have stopped in and helped themselves to a mid-game drink, signing the guest book and leaving a tip at the bar as they go. The owners have taken these developments in gleeful stride, collecting signatures from golf pros, famous artists, authors, St. Andrews pub owners, and TikTok influencers alike.

At every step of conceptualization and construction, we sought to create an architectural response, not only to the Jigger Inn but to the fond experiences and memories created there by our clients. A pub is a meeting place. In the microcosm of a small community, like that of a golf club or a small Scottish village, a pub is a room for life and living, for gathering and shoring up community in a place of casual, constant celebration. And in that spirit, pubs are heavily lived in, lovingly used, and craftily patched when elements begin to wear down. The structure may not be historical in truth, but its interior space conveys a convincing sense that the place has lived a long and storied life.

THE PUB
PRIVATE
MEMBERS ONLY

Champions
Golf Club

SWILCAN
BOX
TODAYS WEATHER
WHO KNOWS?

Weller
RESERVE

Weller
SPECIAL RESERVE

E PUB

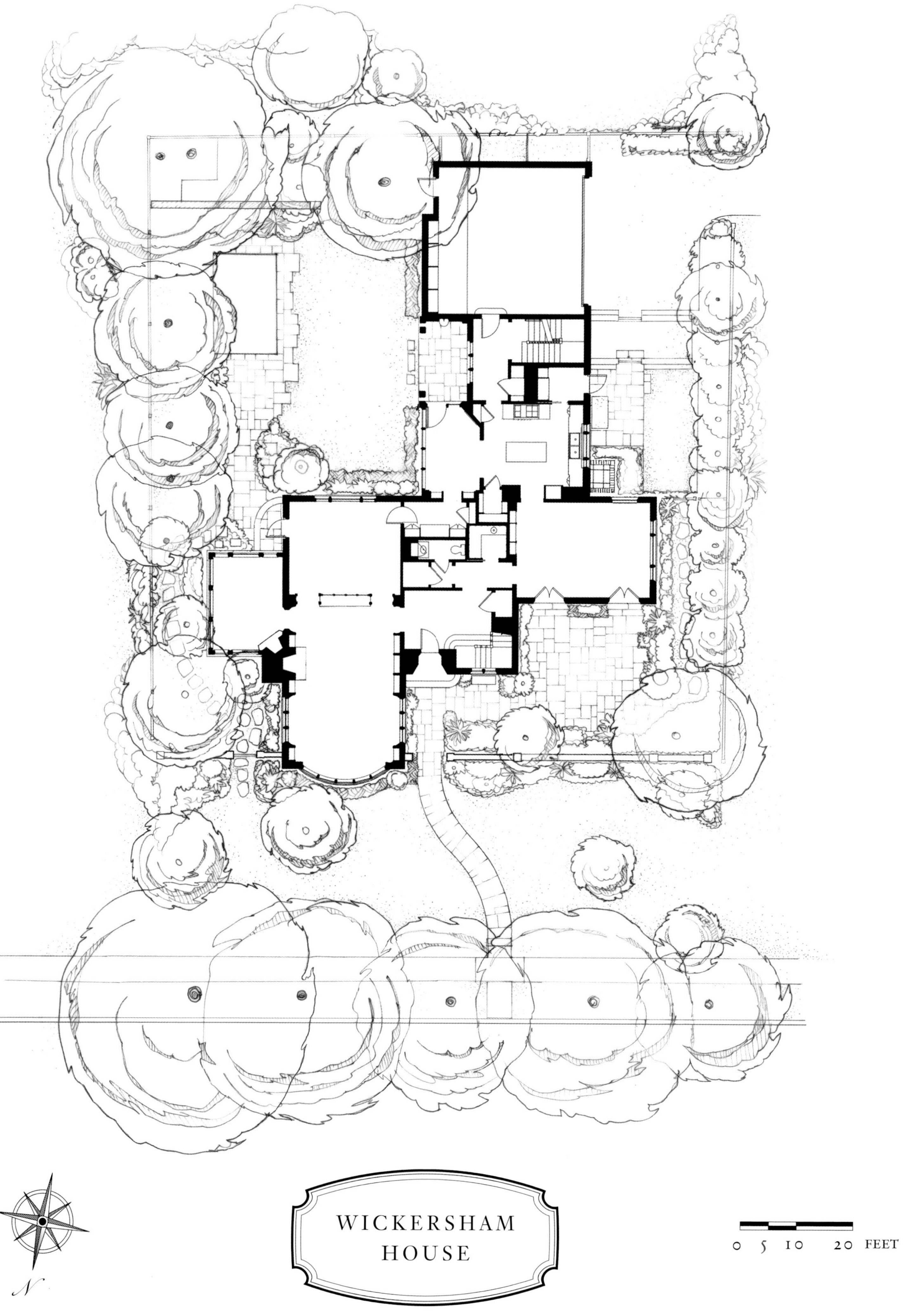
N
WICKERSHAM
HOUSE
0 5 10 20 FEET

V. WICKERSHAM HOUSE

After living on the same lot for several decades, these clients realized that though they had come to love the neighborhood, the needs of their family had evolved beyond the capacity of their current house. After much consideration, they elected to take their existing house down in favor of the freedom offered by constructing a new and ideal home. We designed a home that would respect all of the elements that our clients had grown to appreciate about their location: the modestly scaled, eclectic details of the surrounding houses and the many meaningful relationships that they had cultivated with their neighbors. Our design retained and bolstered these social connections with a respectful, first-development-inspired house that would encourage engaging outdoor relationships between the homeowners and their gardens—a return to the bygone trend of living life in the front yard.

In planning, we found that the property possessed a conveniently located easement that provided access to the nearby cross-street, which would allow for cars to approach the garage exclusively from the rear of the lot, an uncommon feature in the neighborhood of River Oaks. There was no need to shrink the buildable portion of the lot to accommodate a driveway, which allowed us to expand the width of the house to retain a central balance. If we had used that extra width to create a broad, flat, and imposing façade that was clearly bigger than those of the adjacent houses, the project would have failed the cardinal task of blending in. To avoid this, we stepped the massing of the house back from the street in three sections, elevating the middle segment of the roof above the rest. This results in a smaller overall impression of scale. In front of the building, we created a partially enclosed terrace and garden that would relate the house socially to the street. This space, shaded by a verdant pergola and screened by a perforated brick wall, provides a welcoming area for friends and neighbors to spend time together.

We derived the *Z*-shaped plan of the house from the structural ingenuity of homes that predate air-conditioning, which maximized airflow by placing no more than one room across the width of the structure at any given point. This organization, though no longer relied upon for the production of cross-breezes, still allows for the most liberal optimization of natural light within a house. In this design, each major living space has windows on two or three walls. To turn in any direction is to walk toward natural light and a direct view of the lush vegetation beyond. In this manner, the landscape is always present as a component of each room. Our gardens support the house on the interior, just as the interior design leans on the gardens to root a perception of place, and to unify colors on the inside with those present on the outside. Wolf Holden Design Studio is responsible for this thoughtful palette development throughout the home. Their choice of a Voysey-inspired rug to ground the scheme of the living room also functions as a pleasant nod to the gardens visible outside its many windows.

According to the decorators, this Arts and Crafts rug was the departure point for the whole room. Working with the rug's vibrant mood, they began to build an environment that synthesizes and heightens the sensibilities and personal influences of the clients, to make the home feel uniquely theirs. One such influence came from a fond memory that the client held of time spent in her grandfather's green library as a child. "The room tells you what it needs," Wolf remarked, be it family heirlooms, a dash of East Coast charm, Suzani textiles sourced from Turkey, a piece of modern art, or simply the thoughtful reupholstering of the client's original, traditional furnishings.

Over the course of practicing in Houston, we have observed how regrettably easy it can be to ignore the responsibility of designing houses in a way that contributes to the beloved character of River Oaks, especially in the St. John's district, where this house resides. While we're not technically constrained by the long-established list of suggested traditional styles as set forth by the founders (Georgian, Mediterranean, American Federal, etc.), nor expected to shy away from modernism, we've found that an understated, historic scale blends in well and graces the house with a sincere sense of appropriateness. Ultimately, the design of this house is as much about contributing to the city as it is about existing within its own landscape. It can eschew less-than-favorable views for romantic ornamental features of its own creation. Little moments, like a winding stone path, gently arching walls, or a brightly colored door all work to create a modest sense of belonging in an architectural environment where belonging is too often underrated.

FRENCH MINIATURES
THE THOUSAND

ROMANTIC ART

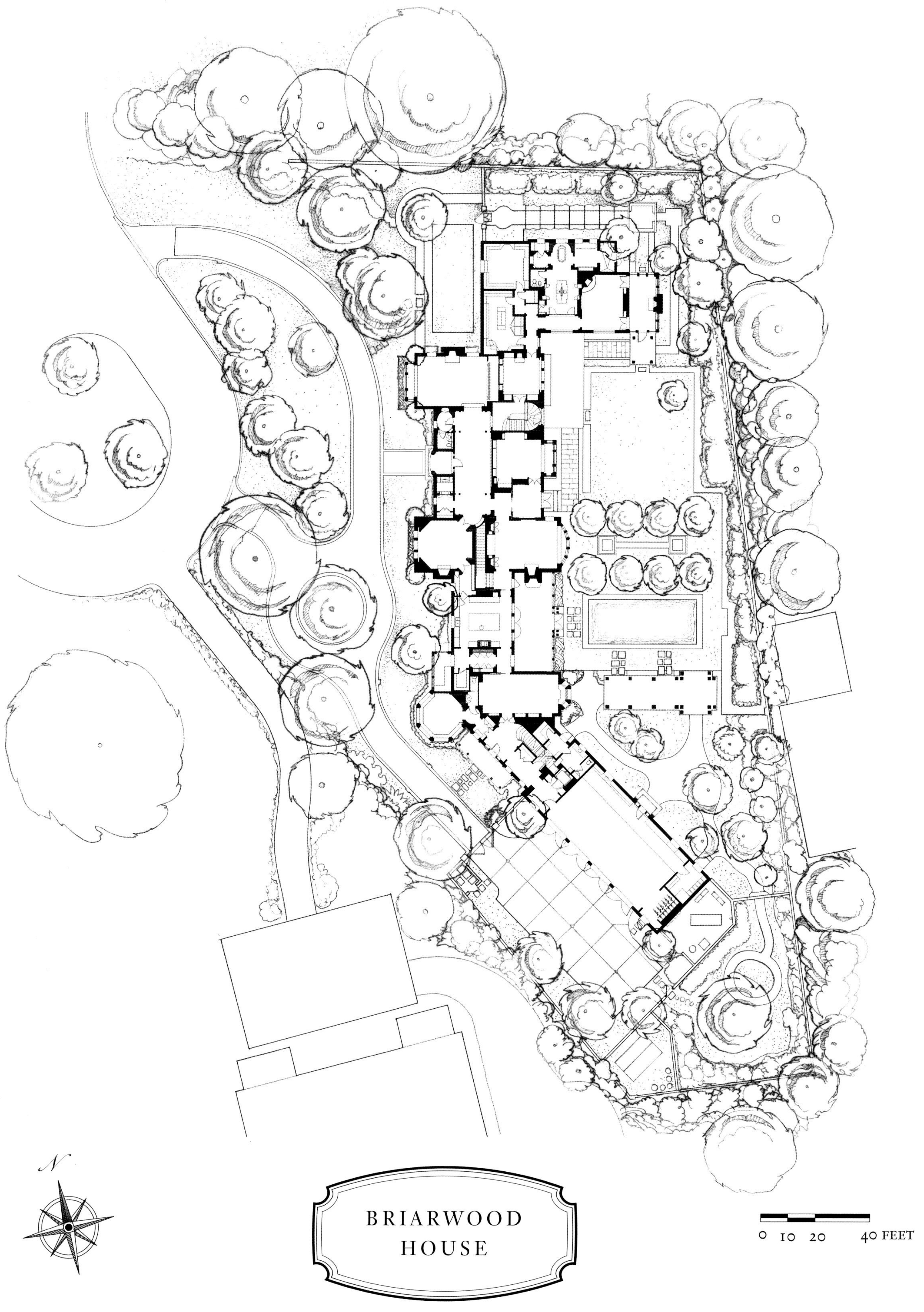
N
BRIARWOOD
HOUSE
0 10 20 40 FEET

VI. BRIARWOOD HOUSE

This River Oaks house is defined by the freedom of eclecticism if nothing else, for inside a conservative, pale gray stucco exterior a vast program of rooms range widely and experiment broadly in the derivation of architectural ideas. In the same way that one might assemble and hang a collection of art that spans eras and movements, so too was this house designed: each choice was inspired in part something that came before. Each room was a response and a generation that desired a life and character consistent with the last set of decisions.

Our first source of inspiration came from the work of Harrie T. Lindeberg, the New York–based architect who is perhaps best known locally for instigating protégé John Staub's move to Houston. Lindeberg's own practice centered on the canny design of country houses that were traditional yet comfortable, possessing rambling footprints, a sensitive handling of materials, and a diverse assemblage of aesthetic influences. He often produced houses that presented a modest front façade, with wings angling off in decidedly different directions than the front of the house would suggest. These would accommodate additional facilities, those not of strict necessity to the main house's traditional program of rooms.

At the start of this project, we were tasked with lacing together a wide variety of programmatic rules on a strangely proportioned, non-rectilinear lot with a narrow entrance due to its position at the end of a cul-de-sac. Following Lindeberg's precedent, we were able to tuck many rooms with distinct functions into a long tail of a lower-lying mass. This maintained a regular front for the house without adding too much bulk on the reverse. Our clients' art collection was referenced frequently throughout the planning process, for several individual pieces or sets of prints required tectonic forethought to create the most ideal architectural envelope for their display. The plan of the entry hall, for example, is largely dictated by the set of twenty large Henri Matisse prints hung on the long wall opposite the front door. A faux skylight illuminates the hall, brightening the artwork and glancing off of the antique parquet floor to bring life to an otherwise shady space.

The adjacent living room wields an austere program of architectural details, save for the elaborately detailed Celtic knot cornice, which acts as a quiet nod to our client's Irish heritage. The decoration of this room consists of an appealing mix of family heirlooms and contemporary art. Traditional architectural details are employed sparingly, like the single paneled wall visible from the entrance hall. It sets up an expectation of formality on the approach to the room that is quickly subverted upon proper entry into the space. The rest of the walls are spartan in their design. Overall, the treatment of this room defers to the character of the furnishings and the colorful art—each room in the house is different in this regard.

The dining room is an elegant, octagonal space crowned with a shining chandelier. Our client's office is stark by comparison, paneled in ebonized walnut with contrasting, by sporadic moments of bright white. The foyer of this space is far tamer, minimally ornamented save for another subtly patterned cornice. At first glance, this cornice appears to be woven together in the style of a second Irish knot, but it is a repeating pattern of diamonds, hearts, clubs, and spades that undulate around the room. Elsewhere in the house, a family room and breakfast nook join together under the pale yellow cover of an English barrel-vaulted ceiling. In combination with a sprawling and steadily unfolding art collection, the variable volumes and styles of these spaces help to draw movement from room to room—the promise of an unpredictable architectural experience lies in waiting beyond each consecutive doorway.

Our equally expansive range of landscape details plays a significant role in the grounding and justification of the large house. A crafty jumble of gardens flows around vine-covered arches that shade gravel walks. Pergolas offer respite for sunbathers. Symmetrical rows of trees bracket an inlaid fountain near the pool. On the edges of the house, flowers creep up trellised walls, and stepping stones set into grass meander back and forth, culminating in a whimsical garden gate that leads to a secret, walled lawn at the southern end of the house.

JAMES TURRELL
TEXAS ARTISTS TODAY
JAMES TURRELL
NEW WINE
French Impressionism
LUXURY HOUSES
EDWARD HOPPER
ROTHKO
SOUTINE
SOUTINE
Matisse Cut-outs
Matisse Jazz

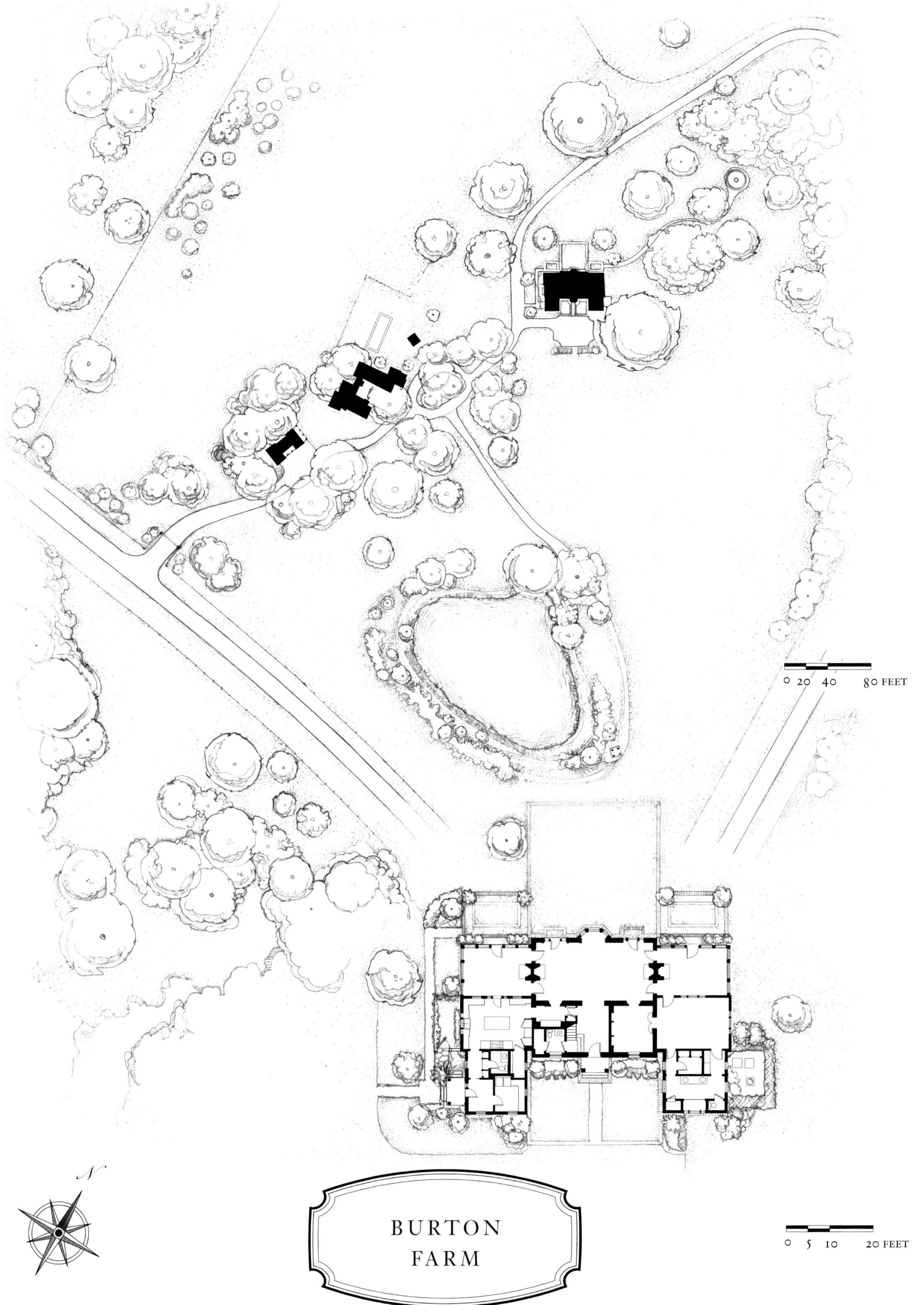

0 20 40 80 FEET
N
BURTON
FARM
0 5 10 20 FEET

VII. BURTON FARM

In the middle of the nineteenth century, a flood of German immigrants came rushing up from the Gulf of Galveston to the southernmost edge of the Texas Hill Country. A majority of these hopeful souls settled along the Balcones scarp and set their hearts on cultivating farmlands of similar or superior caliber to those they had left behind in Europe. As they doggedly plowed the region's inhospitable soil, farmers tilled from their fields a seemingly endless supply of limestone rocks, which were quickly identified as a readily accessible building material for their new homes. These field stones were stacked in overlapping layers to form rectilinear walls, and their surfaces were plastered over with stucco to waterproof the porous stone. Thus began the era of the German-Texas rock house, which has remained a reputable building precedent in the very same region where our clients purchased a small farm several years ago.

Their newly acquired acreage was not a typical homestead, for it ran alongside El Camino Real, a prominent prehistoric road that holds a significant place in the annals of Texas history. Mounted on the edge of a small escarpment, the high point of their low ridge possessed heroic forty-mile views to the east and west. The original farmhouse that our clients sought to replace had not capitalized on the grand vistas and strong breezes of the ridgeline, an oversight we put to rights with our new site. We situated the house in an opportune gap amid a bosque of mature oak trees, later adding new gravel roads to support the placement of the house in relation to the larger property, as it stood on a hill at a distance from the original infrastructure.

One local home, a Saxon replica from the 1850s located in the nearby town of Round Top, set a foundational precedent for our final design. It was a small, two-story, stone and plaster house with two-foot-thick walls and a wooden shake roof, modeled after the stonemason's own home in Germany. To scale up this vernacular historical construction, we based our house around a slightly larger central block with thick stucco walls. Unburdened by the narrow scope of earlier technology, we chose to imitate the look of German-Texan practices through the layering of wood, concrete, and plaster, in a modern allusion to the precedent. To expand the house's program without compromising the integrity of the site, we attached symmetrical wooden wings on either side of the central core to hold extra bedrooms, create porches, and accompanying facilities. The reduced scale and material shift of these posterior elements make the central block look contrastingly robust and demonstrative, as if it harkens back to a prior era of construction. Inside one of these rear porches, a plaster fireplace slopes gently upward and resolves into the room's simple white crown molding, a manner of handling materials that quietly draws attention back to the tectonics of the house.

Upon observation of the larger property, it is evident that the house's uncompromising frontal symmetry and relatively large scale allow it to hold sway over such a prominent location, set as it is amid many equally commanding trees. Notably, the house's two main elevations diverge in prominence and personality on the approach and the reverse: the rear is purposefully grander than the front, an atypical feature in any residence, country or otherwise. It may seem incongruous, but these forms work to accommodate the visual contrast of witnessing the house from the foot of a five-hundred-yard driveway versus a forty-mile overland view.

Inside, simple and natural materials work to reinforce an overarching narrative of traditional construction. Oak floors, beams, and the same white plaster that characterizes the exterior lend a sense of familiar propriety to the space. The interior decoration is correspondingly unselfconscious. Traditional fabrics upholster comfortable sofas and chairs to provide an easy complement to the mature, honest expression of the architecture. The furniture is laid out symmetrically, in keeping with the balance of the house, and the floor plan is a simple one, leaving no room for disorientation. The furnishings turn the mind outwards, not inwards. They reflect a house that encourages the occupants to truly be present in the surroundings, to easily and consistently take in the impressive views that render the property so unique.

John James Audubon in the West
A. HAYS TOWN

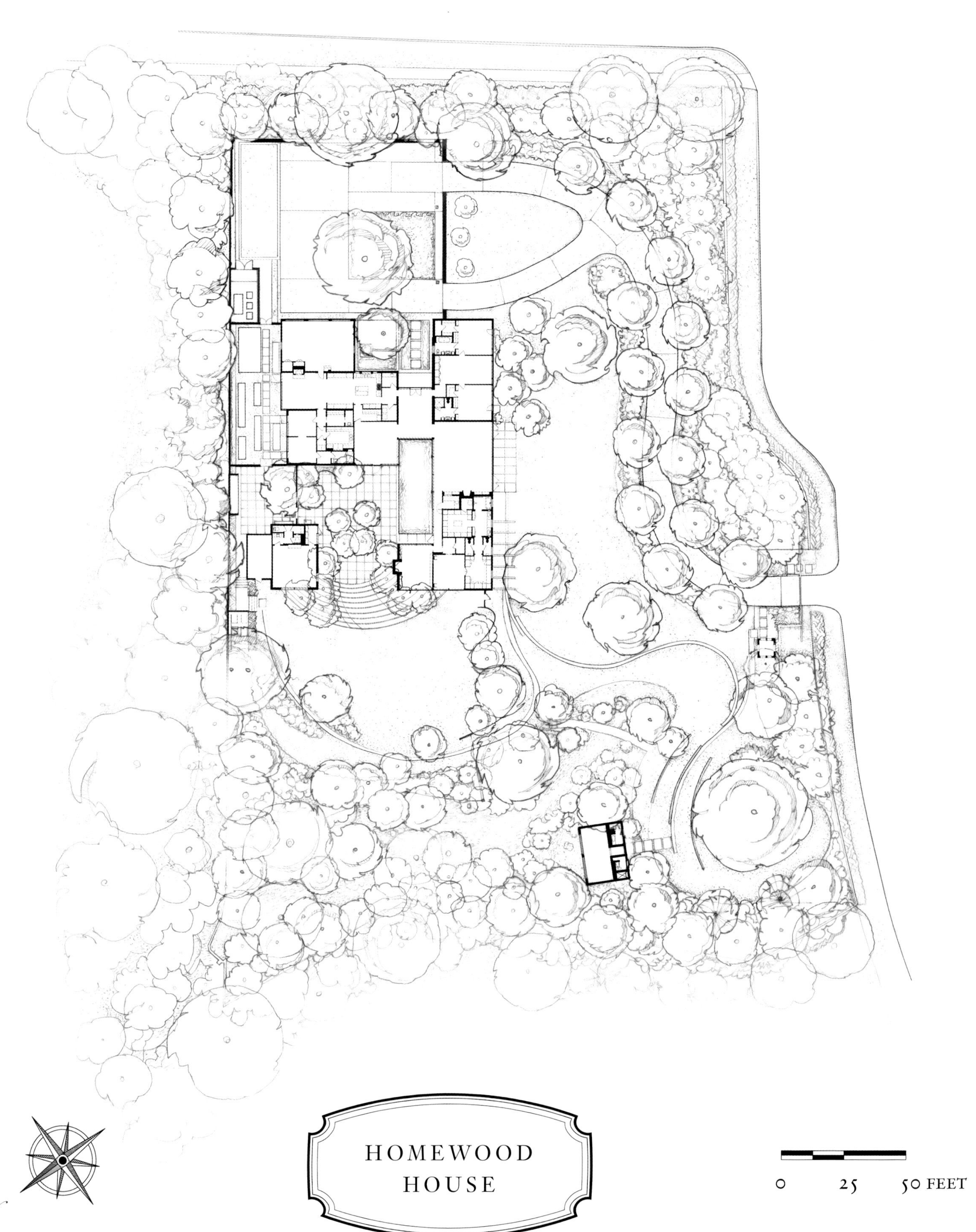

N
HOMEWOOD
HOUSE
0
25
50 FEET

VIII. HOMEWOOD HOUSE

It takes a fearless client to initiate a fearless project, and this recent renovation benefited from brave choices throughout. Houstonian architect Hugo Neuhaus designed this sprawling single-story villa for his family in 1950, just two years after Philip Johnson's nearby Menil house. In the decades since the architect's death, the property has changed hands several times. Each successive change brought a new chance to remodel the historic landmark, but the accumulation began to leach the site of its purity. Working in conjunction with Reed Hilderbrand Landscape Architecture, we performed a series of adjustments that we felt would serve the needs of our clients without sacrificing Neuhaus's original vision.

Modernist architecture of the type Neuhaus and Johnson practiced was heavily inspired by the work of Ludwig Mies van der Rohe, specifically those projects which neutralized relationships between the inside and outside. After reorienting the original driveway to the calmer of the two neighboring streets, we began to establish coherence and continuity between the house and its garden to support this legacy of interconnectivity. Leading up to the front door, several wide steps of pink terrazzo act as a floating bridge across a shallow pool of water, which in turn sits on an axis with the swimming pool at the center of the plan. Water unifies the house and landscape by establishing an elemental motif that carries through the walls of the property.

Inside the U-shaped compound, we stripped back previous layers of renovation to reveal the original brick walls that tie the entryway to the material language of the exterior. Much of our interior work spruced, neatened, and reestablished clarity where it had been lost, leaving plenty of space for our clients to take over the house and make it their own.

Our client has worked with several interior designers on this project, and each wave continued to evolve their voice, even while our client was clear on maintaining the original language of the house. When original materials could no longer be matched exactly, she worked to respect Neuhaus's vision and carry it through to the modern day. Overall, our client wished to live in a home whose beauty did not eclipse its functionality. Kids, dogs, and friends who like red wine are all welcome here, freed from the fear of making a mess. Plenty has been done to respect Houston's American country house tradition, but far fewer residents respond to the International Style of modernism brought here by Johnson. Given this disparity, our client's choice to raise her family in one of Houston's modernist classics is a gesture of respect and commitment to the city's past and present culture.

In combination with the cultivation of an extensive contemporary art collection, contributions from Summer Thornton and Studio Shamshiri have resulted in a bright, colorful, and interactive environment that remains open to growth and change. The living room, for one, wells with light and life. Deep red bookshelves contrast splendidly with pale, curved sofas and a vivid green rug. A custom David Wiseman ceiling installation shrinks the perceived scale of the room, establishing a surprisingly romantic and intimate atmosphere for a space with so many floor-to-ceiling windows. To the right of the fireplace, short red velvet curtains open onto a hidden pocket bar, which shimmers from the light reflected off its disco-ball-tiled walls. The end of the adjacent hallway glows with the shifting colors of a James Turrell light piece, turning the wall into an extension of the artwork.

On the far side of the house, we designed a new outbuilding to hold a miniature spa, complete with a resistance pool, hot and cold plunge pools, and a sauna. These circular plunge pools are centered beneath individual skylights, creating private moments of shimmering light inside the otherwise hard marble chamber. Just outside, the carefully groomed lawn slopes quickly downward, where it meets with the wild landscape of the nearby bayou. Large grass steps engage the enclosed terrazzo terrace with the property beyond, directing sight and movement across a small ravine to one of the few entirely new features of our renovation. Here, far behind the house, we designed a small, transparent pavilion that can function independently as a guest room or office space. This structure blends in neatly into the landscape thanks to its sparse palette of glass and charred wood. This pavilion is graced with a clear view of the entire villa, situated snugly within a grand landscape that deftly complements its highly linear architectural language.

7
WINDOWS

CHINATI
DAUM
KEN FULK
TOM FORD

CAMPARI
Maker's Mark

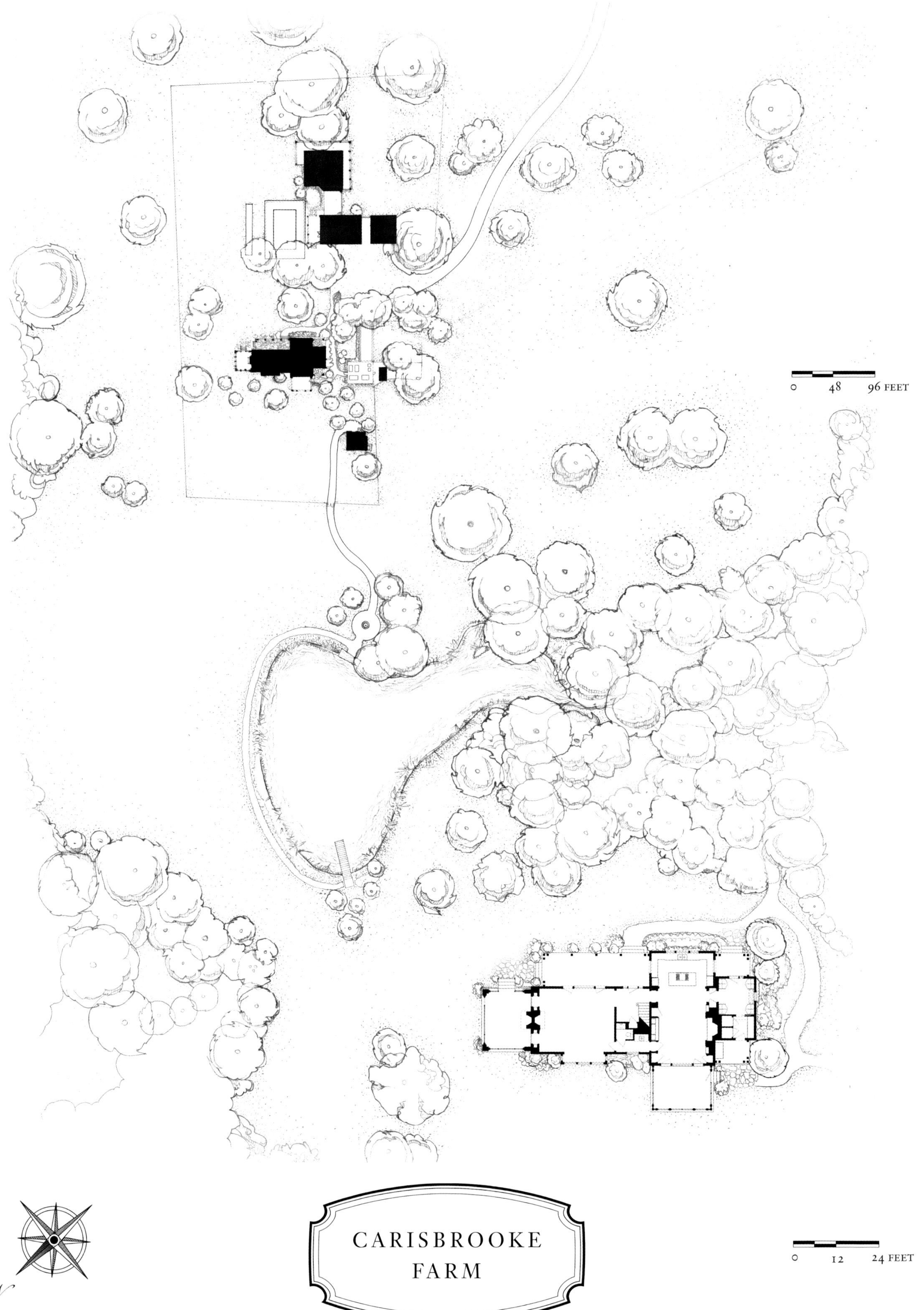
0 48 96 FEET
N
CARISBROOKE
FARM
0 12 24 FEET

IX. CARISBROOKE FARM

When the father who commissioned this project first came to us, it was on behalf of his full-fledged children and their young families. Our client sought to build an addition on his rural Texas compound, in collaboration with one of his daughters, that would allow the growing ranks of their family to enjoy the countryside together by proactively meeting the need for less-cramped accommodations. We began by considering how best to establish an amicable relationship between the new construction and its surroundings, namely, the collection of white clapboard ranch-style buildings that predated our project's development on the site. They set forth a clear aesthetic to which any future work that wished to blend in peaceably must observe and respond. Our adaptation of these core characteristics allowed the new house to contribute comfortably to the ethos of the property without becoming an overly dominating presence.

The residence was built in the spirit of an old Texas farmhouse, both in its choice of materials and the simplicity of form and function as guiding principles that support an outdoor-oriented, pared-down lifestyle. The structure sits on the steepest edge of a tree-studded hilltop, overlooking a small lake and its surrounding pastures. Though it rests on the same plane as the main house and its adjoining pool, garage, and tack room, we distanced the new house from the edge of the preexisting compound to lend a modicum of privacy to its inhabitants. A vegetable garden and a discreet exercise building bracket one end of the house, relating the new construction to the larger property's established pattern of grouping multiple buildings of differing scales. These smaller structures lend the house a sense of space and presence when it might have otherwise stood alone.

We designed the initial arrival sequence to engage the most dynamic and ideal experience of the house—encouraging visitors to leave cars behind in a shady gravel parking area and stroll along a designated footpath that travels under the canopy of several mature live oaks. This treesy approach leads graciously to the front door, whose placement on the end of a porch populated with rocking chairs welcomes newcomers with the prospect of a scenic view, waiting just around the corner. Since the white wooden walls of the exterior set a prominent visual narrative for the house that roots the building in place among its fellows, it was next necessary to carry a similarly unifying narrative through to the architecture of the interior, via its simply paneled white walls. In doing so, the experience of moving back and forth from landscape to house becomes a fluid transition, comforting in its local predictability and overall coherence. Inside, large communal living and dining rooms occupy the first floor, while bedrooms and other private facilities are housed above. A long, well-lit hallway runs the length of the second floor, culminating in an airy sleeping porch that holds two pillow-strewn loveseats and a partner's desk. This private space allows our clients to take full advantage of the property's best feature: expansive views in three cardinal directions.

Overall, the massing of the house, with its variable heights, unenclosed spaces, and lack of bilateral symmetry collaborates well with the form of the hilltop from above and below, inside and out. The rear façade of the house creates a far less personal relationship with the viewer than the frontal approach along the top of the hill. This lakeside elevation purposefully appears much larger, to better suit its prominent siting. The orientation and elevation of the plan respect the nuances of the topography, instead of enforcing disruptions onto them. The front door is stationed on a flat section of the earth while elsewhere, below the two-tiered porch structure on the far side of the house, the land begins to fall away, lending a greater sense of height and prominence to the vistas that extend outward in three directions simultaneously.

PERFECT PORCHES
THE ROOM OUTSIDE
Book of Texas Birds

SWEET—CORN
AMERICAN ART

ARTISTS IN EXILE
Ansel Adams

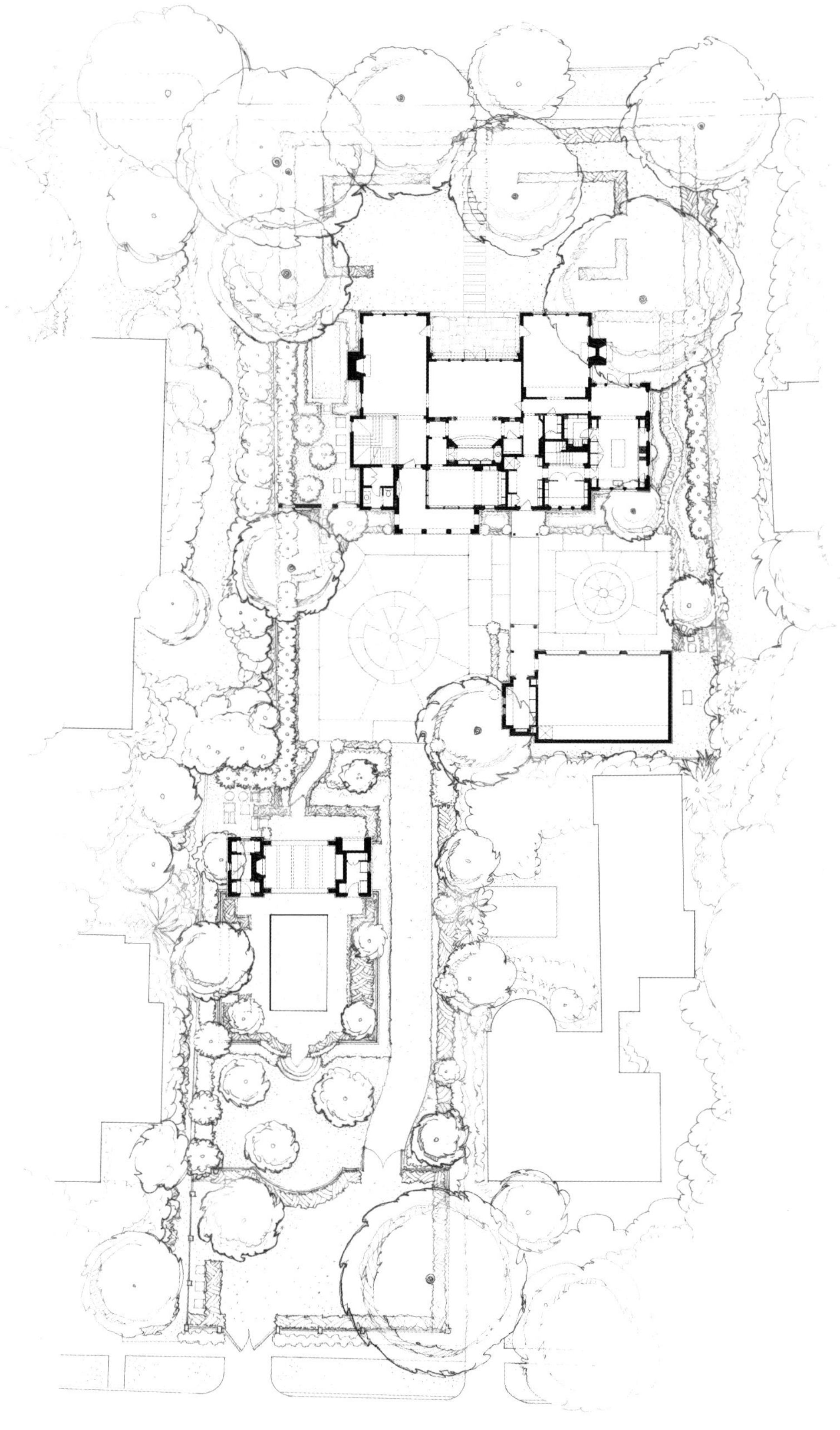

INVERNESS
HOUSE

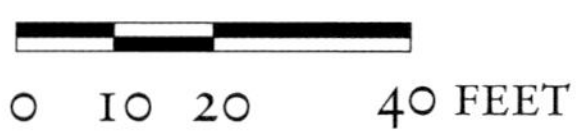

0 10 20 40 FEET

X. INVERNESS HOUSE

The client, a family with two teenage daughters, had acquired two long and narrow lots directly abutting one another on their respective short ends, each facing a different, curving, River Oaks street. After presenting us with a brief for the desired program and social functions of their house, we were released to explore the constraints and advantages of working with a property of such an unorthodox shape. How could two lots and two street addresses come together to sustain one house without disrupting the integrity of either property, while simultaneously enhancing the benefits of both? The answer, we found, lay within a site plan that drew equal inspiration from English country estates as it did from the felicity of its location.

When we viewed this bifurcated (yet jointly functioning) entity, we realized that the coupling of two properties presented a rare gift: the main house could be set with its back against the front of the larger lot, using the full length and width of both lots to create a grand, processional entry onto a property quietly removed from the ordinary grid of the surrounding neighborhood. The resulting view from the entry street is unconventional. Since it was impossible to establish a clear line of sight into the heart of the property from the sidewalk or driveway, uniform hedgerows briefly reveal a small auto court and the roof of an undefined outbuilding en route to the main house, but much of their purpose and character remains veiled.

The primary axis of the joined properties is only revealed once a visitor has progressed past the front gate, which is stationed at the back of the public auto court. Once through the gate, visitors must traverse a shallow S-curve in the drive before catching a proper glimpse of the main house. Then the procession begins: down a long gravel lane, past hedges and small gardens that shield a discreet pool complex, through a second auto court set beside a covered walkway and garage, and under a triple archway—there the entry finally lies. The anecdotal experiences of such a measured, grand entry foster the impression that you've left River Oaks behind, slipping sideways onto some bucolic country lane in search of a commanding estate.

When given liberties to devise the visual language of the house, we gravitated toward the country estates of Surrey, whose painted and unpainted white-brick façades struck us as the type of design that might have predated a neighborhood like River Oaks. With a wythe of brick facing, we imitated the tectonics of those load-bearing brick walls to take advantage of their unique visual dynamics, such as turned bricks and unpainted quoins. On the northern façade, we spanned two brick masses with wooden brackets and coursed siding, opening up the dining room wall to allow for as much northern light as possible. For a suggestion of consequence and history, we left these brackets tethered on an exterior plane. Their separation implies the preexistence of a once-open loggia that was later filled in with a wall of glass, maintaining a sense of transparency with the garden beyond.

The main axis of sight continues upon entering the house by way of the front door, proceeding through the entry hall, past the stairwell, under a second archway, and into the living room, whereupon the gaze is directed out the back windows, over the hedge, and across the street to a lush, green focal point. The highly reflective living room ceiling, decorator Suzanne Kasler's contribution, initiates a moment of transference from exterior to interior through the glow of a pale green light. Every room on the first floor borrows a view from the gardens across the street, save for the two private offices. This plan only works because the house is technically oriented with its back to that street, there being no formal entry on the north side of the main lot. And yet, if you were to throw open the paned-glass doors of the dining room onto the stone terrace beyond, the flow of the house could reverse entirely, and the back could convert sociably into the front. Such an eccentricity, a house that flows forward and backward in equal measure with the formal and informal rooms reversed, is an idiosyncratic trait reinforced and celebrated by this site plan.

A WANDERING EYE
LISA FINE NEAR & FAR INTERIORS I LOVE
THE PARISIANS
TASTEMAKERS AT HOME
Flammarion
ASSOULINE
VALENTINO AT THE EMPEROR'S TABLE

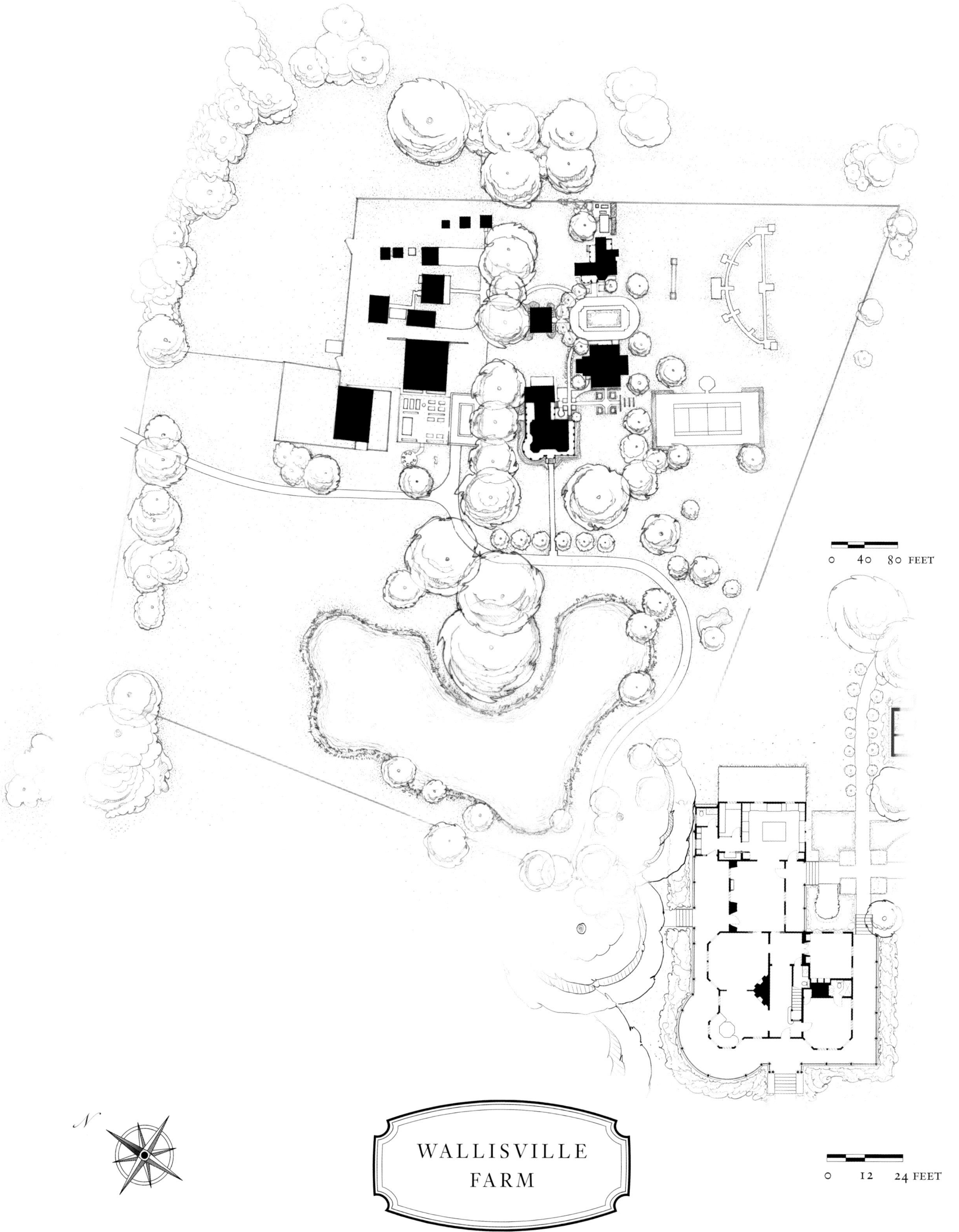
0 40 80 FEET
N
WALLISVILLE
FARM
0 12 24 FEET

XI. WALLISVILLE FARM

Though it has faced nearly two centuries of unrelenting disaster, this property, which overlooks the historic community of Wallisville, Texas, has refused to succumb to the calamitous fates of its neighbors. The property first entered into history in 1836, when, in a shining moment of local triumph, the Mexican dictator Antonio López de Santa Anna was briefly held captive on this very hilltop, after his defeat at the Battle of San Jacinto. Darker moments came in the ensuing decades when multiple category-four hurricanes made landfall along the Gulf Coast, carrying their paths of destruction many miles inland. The hurricane of 1915 nearly erased Wallisville from the map. Over a period of two days, all but eight houses fell victim to the storm. Hundreds of townspeople sheltered within this property's large Victorian house as they fled from the rising waters and racing winds. In 1966, the nearby town was unwillingly purchased by the federal government in preparation for the construction of a reservoir, and many more homes were destroyed as a result.

Our clients, the current generation of owners, wished to revitalize and modernize the surviving property for their growing family, without ridding it of its rich myth and history. In answering their requests, we sought to create a pastoral oasis that retains the function of a farm when necessary but gives way to more visually compelling relationships between buildings and landscape wherever possible. First, we reorganized the lengthy entry sequence to create a scenic approach that winds around a newly expanded lake, cut through a line of mature trees, and comes to rest in a parking court adjacent to the fenced-in complex of the main house. On the other side of this court, next to preexisting barns and functional outbuildings, we built an extensive vegetable garden and greenhouse where our clients grow produce year-round.

From this point, the approach to the house comes through opening the gate of a rolling white-picket fence and passing through an impressive row of live oaks, whose massive trunks and moss-strewn branches lend the house an invaluable sense of gravitas. Their soaring canopies allow an uncharacteristically tall building to appear well-suited to an otherwise low-lying landscape.

Our remodel of this house was performed in conjunction with the efforts of interior designer Anne Grandinetti, with Ashby Collective, to respect the stylistic integrity of the house's heritage while elegantly dispersing a contemporary flair. We brought in materials that would reflect the spirit of genuine craftsmanship, like the properly burnished plaster walls in the dining room, or the specially commissioned mural in the entry hall, onto which Houston's Rusty Arena painted pastoral scenes that subtly feature the surrounding property. These rooms exemplify the house's soulful-yet-somber interior color palette, which we borrowed from the dapple-gray shadows and darkly furrowed trunks of the surrounding live oaks.

Progressing outside, we addressed the property's need for an engaging and sociable focal point through the addition of a pool. At the far end of this pool, pleasantly rolling pastures begin to overtake diligently tended lawns and gardens. The preexisting fence obscured these idyllic views, so we built a ha-ha to serve as an equally functional yet discreet barrier, one that would drop out of sight below the level of the pool. Between the pool and the house, we designed an entirely new pavilion to transition between these two spaces. This orangerie-like outbuilding is rendered with a language complementary to that of the main house, for fluid visual continuity. On the remaining sides of the pool, we relocated and refurbished two of the property's existing structures—an independent guest house, and a functional one-room schoolhouse, or office space, depending on the needs of the day. A series of gardens and meandering brick paths mediate between these many reconfigurations of landscape and architecture, reestablishing an attitude of constancy and maturity that unifies the property.

INTIMATE CHANEL
VOGUE THE COVERS
MARFA FLIGHTS
THE LIGHT OF ISTANBUL
EYES OVER AFRICA

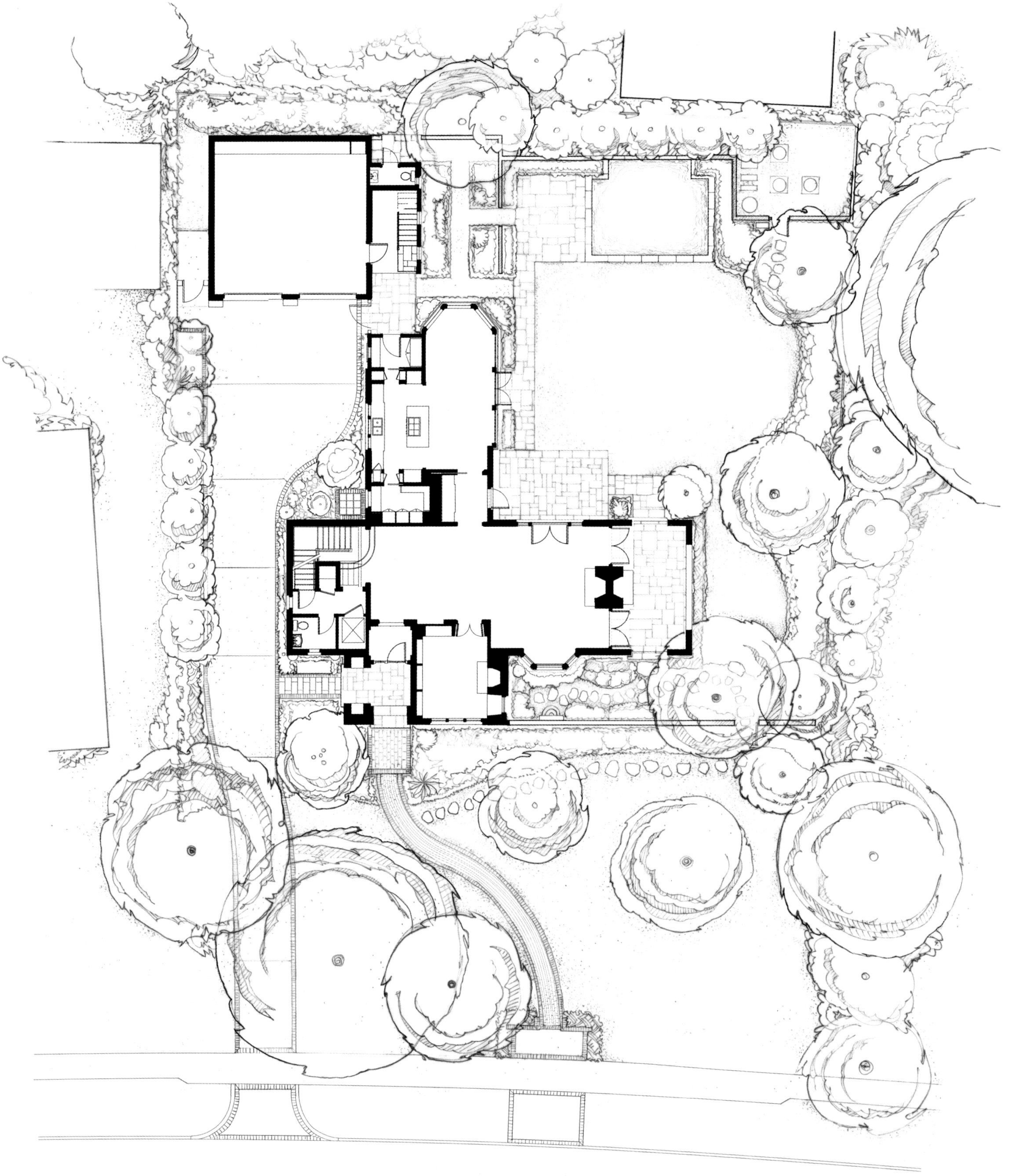

N

PINE VALLEY HOUSE

0 4 8 16 FEET

XII. PINE VALLEY HOUSE

The neighboring architecture, which set the tone for this mid-block Houston residence, was modest and well-mannered, above all else. The architects of those extant first-generation houses demonstrated a confident and familiar manipulation of traditional architectural language, in keeping with the original philosophy of the neighborhood; all buildings contribute peaceably and proportionally to the betterment of the whole. Upon deciding to downsize, our clients were drawn to this particular property because they appreciated the retention of that principled atmosphere. We sought to fold our new construction into this mix with a scaled-down plan that satisfies the contemporary tastes of our clients in a synthesis of style that no first-generation house could have attained.

We found that the mid-nineteenth-century English Arts and Crafts movement is uniquely capable of building a stylized bridge between a traditional exterior and a modern interior, the two poles of our design. The Arts and Crafts movement focused on generating beauty and meaning from the artful expression of ordinary building materials, while simultaneously solidifying a connection between their new construction and its surroundings. This, too, is what we sought to do. We drew upon the movement's use of well-proportioned solid forms, asymmetrical building compositions, vernacular references, textural expression of materials, stress on horizontal lines, engagement with nature, and willful impressions of the craftsman, to name a few clear points of reference.

We applied several of these principles on the exterior of the house alone. First, the facing is split along a low horizontal line, with the denser of two visible materials grounding the lower section. This, in combination with a twenty-foot cornice that falls well below the house's two-story height restriction, works to reduce the perceived verticality of the frontage. Treating the façade in this manner allows a building with a larger overall footprint to slip in comfortably beside its smaller neighbors without drawing attention to itself. On a more personal level, the exterior features various small-scale details that draw upon the history of craftsmanship to fashion an imagined, experiential relationship with the singular aesthetic of the builder. Think of the organically carved wooden balcony railing or the arched brick entryway with its charmingly empty niches . . . Altogether, the façade of the house reads as traditionally modest, with its simple gable and unembellished bricklaying. The street face boasts few windows, a common balancing tactic for a house of this kind. On the back of the house, several full walls of windows open up onto the garden, lending views, light, and increased ease of engagement with nature to the private corner.

Functionally, the leading role of an entry hall begins before the front door is even opened, as it's approached by a bricked-in outdoor threshold with a white-painted, wooden-paneled ceiling. Our use of contrasting materials, colors, and textures in this context lends an unconscious impression of a conventional indoor hall, even before crossing over the formal threshold of the house.

Our contemporary plan presents itself upon entry. Two formal spaces—the dining room and living room—unfold openly onto one another at the foot of the stairs. The stair itself is a robust, visually dynamic manifestation of pure craft. Solid and sculptural, with posts and handrail cut on the bias, the element draws the eye upward and casts the mind back to a time when craftsmen engaged in design on a complex and intimate level. Large windows set high into the wall above the stairs send a warm glow of natural light filtering down the treads, across the foot of the stairs, and into the windowless dining room. A dining room in the center of a plan is entirely nontraditional, but multiple sources of borrowed light, like that of the lofty second floor and the many living room windows at the back of the house, work together to create an atmosphere entirely suited to low-lit dinners with friends and family.

Given the relatively shallow rise of the house's second story, any excess ornamentation on the first-floor ceilings would have shrunk that perception of height even further. Nevertheless, the ceilings did want some element of texture, especially in the formal rooms, whose walls were minimally detailed with wainscoting and little else. To mediate these needs, we created a bas-relief ceiling, but purposefully left the origin of its surface texture open to multiple interpretations. Its streamlined presence enhances the house's modern feeling, subtly—is it an additive pattern or the visual tectonics carrying over from the construction of the second floor? Mindful details such as these contribute powerfully to the personal experience of moving through new construction, with or without prior knowledge of a historical, architectural context.

WINSLOW HOMER
TEXAS

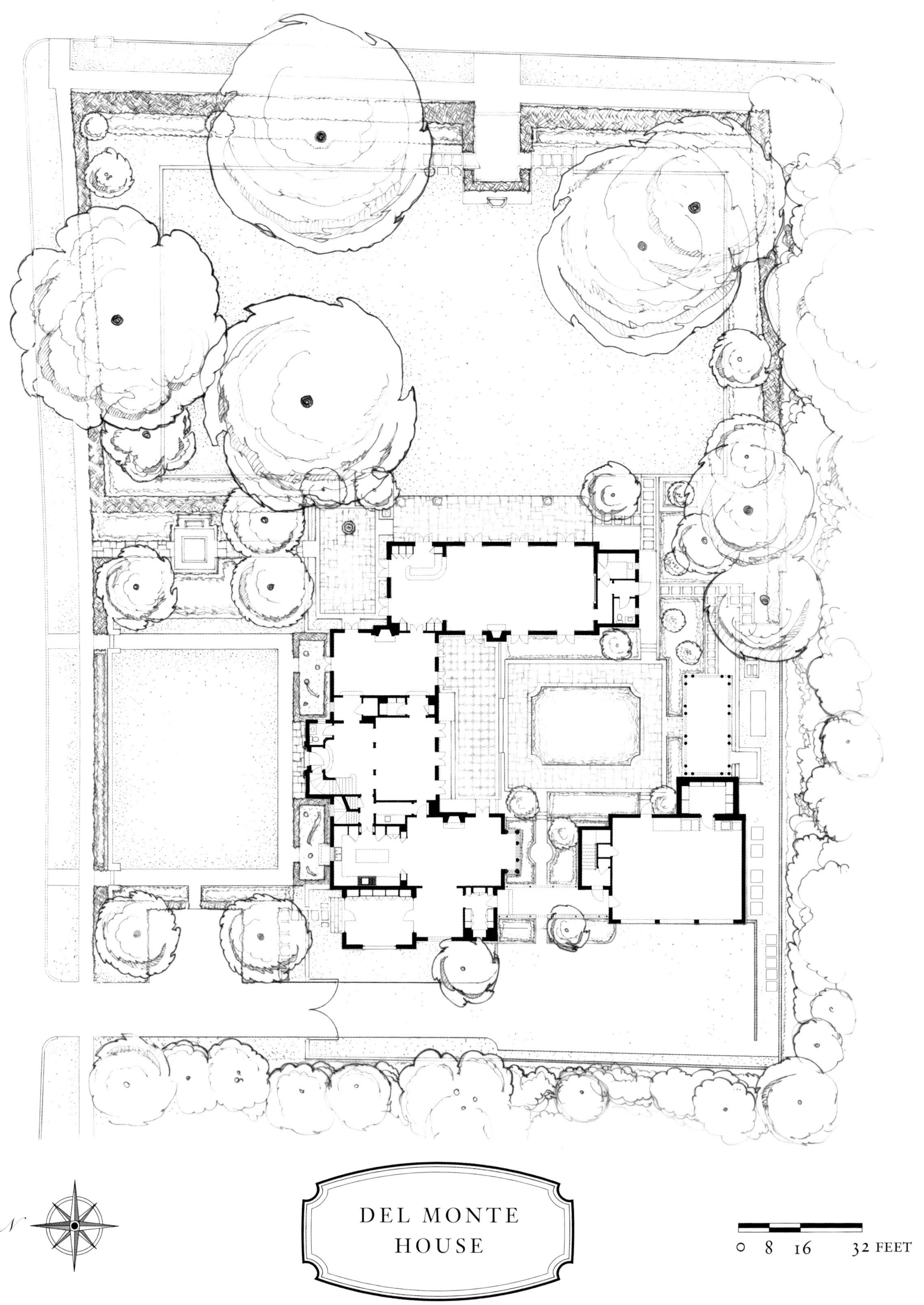
DEL MONTE
HOUSE
N
0 8 16 32 FEET

XIII. DEL MONTE HOUSE

Each first-generation house in Houston's most affluent neighborhood, River Oaks, was modeled after a traditional style of architecture, forming a uniquely eclectic and American mix. Georgian-inspired houses coexisted harmoniously with Spanish Revival, American Colonial with Mediterranean, provincial French with early Republic. When the Hogg brothers first purchased several hundred acres of Houston property in the 1920s and developed it speculatively under the River Oaks Corporation, the assemblage of architectural styles that they encouraged was meant to entice and inspire prospective homeowners. They felt that these styles were capable of gracefully expressing individuality, while simultaneously setting forth a collective aspirational tone for the neighborhood. These lofty goals presented no small amount of work for a pioneering real estate program, and yet the widely successful efforts of those early architects and developers still work their charm on the neighborhood's gently curving streets nearly a century later.

One such first-generation house, in a provincial French style, was purchased by a young couple with Texas roots who had recently moved to Houston from New York. Seeking to preserve their new home's authentic street presence, our clients did not engage us to start anew, but rather to add a garage, extend a wing, rework the landscape, and renovate the interiors, paving the way for the decorative work of local interior designer Randy Powers.

The house came with a distinguishing quirk: an undeveloped corner lot anchored the east side of the property; this created a spacious buffer between the house proper and the prominent thoroughfare of River Oaks Boulevard. The boulevard, as affluent in character as the neighborhood in which it resides, leads to the River Oaks Country Club. The adjacent lots are characterized by large, classical houses with huge setbacks that visually support the tone of the street. The discreet separation of this house from the status quo of the block was a point of intrigue for our clients, rather than a cause for consternation. If safeguarded, the lot would provide a precious belt of green between the drive and the front of the house. Their young children could grow up playing outside to their heart's content without disrupting neighbors or putting themselves on display for the highly trafficked street.

First, we planted a robust hedge around the expansive grassy lawn that borders River Oaks Boulevard. Into this hedge, we set a grand, formal entryway, a pedestrian entrance that could welcome partygoers directly onto the large outdoor gathering space, without requiring them to pass through the main house. We added and adjusted several additional landscape features to reinforce the eccentricity of this layout, like a new U-shaped courtyard at the rear edge of the house, or the reorganization of the Del Monte Drive–facing front lawn. Reshaping this area into an unbroken patch of grass both formalizes the preexisting façade and forces guests to choose from one of two new points of entry: they may skirt around the right side and enter into the client's office, or they may proceed to the left and gain direct access to the courtyard, lawn, and the extended wing that now houses several comfortable sitting areas and an elegant freestanding bar.

With the exception of an entirely new garage, we were able to redefine the manner in which our clients wished to live with a series of customized gestures. Inside the house, Powers's lush interiors are quietly bolstered by a suitably refined program of architectural details, such as antique oak cabinets and ceiling beams that unify and enliven an otherwise cool, marbled kitchen. Upstairs, decorative dormer windows illuminate the hallways of the main house and the private rooms above the garage with a bright eastern light. To visually communicate the clients' overall goals, we rooted this renovation in deference to the larger property's public reputation, without sacrificing the individual comfort or privacy of those who dwell within.

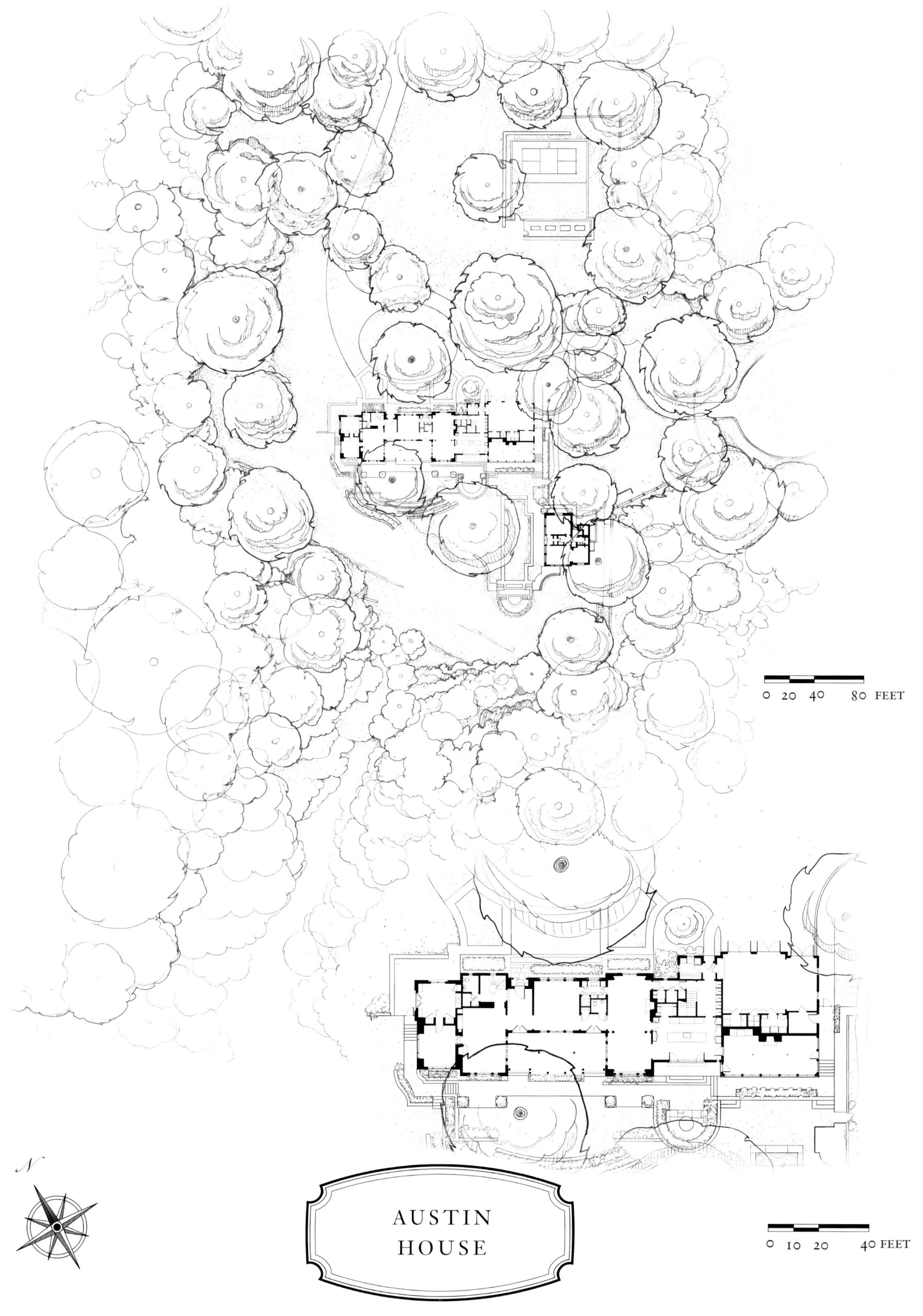
0 20 40 80 FEET
N
AUSTIN
HOUSE
0 10 20 40 FEET

XIV. AUSTIN HOUSE

These nine acres of densely treed property sit on a hill overlooking the lively waters of Lake Austin and are perched high above the sprawling urban chaos of the surrounding city. To find an intact parcel of land this large inside any major city is a rare feat in this day and age; equally surprising was the discovery that a lot of this size did not allow for nearly limitless design possibilities. The parameters of this house were prescribed, practically to the foot, by the natural environment surrounding it. When our clients first acquired this uncommon property, they assumed the responsibility of stewardship over the landscape, which is no easy task in this region. Trees in Austin, Texas, are highly protected, and the rigid rules that keep them safe means construction must that dance around their far-reaching root systems and voluminous canopies. Our design occupies the only area on the lot that was free of these massive live oaks, and was a space once occupied by a previous home.

Our clients were drawn to a mix of aesthetic references that ranged from the squarely traditional to the decidedly modern. With these in mind, we designed a house with a conventionally symmetrical, privacy-establishing front façade that dissolves into a largely transparent rear that faces the lake. On this side, wide French doors open onto a series of terraces overlooking a serene swimming pool. The property drops off steeply to the other side, allowing for uninterrupted views of the landscape beyond. Austin was founded on the banks of the Colorado River; as the city developed, dams were built to interrupt its flow, resulting in a series of small lakes that bisect Austin's sprawling footprint. The most central of these is Lake Austin, the locus of this property's view. Elevated sites are a rare find in Texas; elevation within a densely populated city even more so, so our clients were eager to capitalize on this extraordinary location.

At the back of the house, a stretch of lawn rolls toward the treeline opposite the pool house. Thickly forested hills drift up on either side, framing a shining swath of the river as it winds its way between them. Above, the bright Texas sky looms as large as ever, uniting the landscape under its sunny expanse. To take full advantage of this prospect, we created a long, shallow plan, where an enfilade of rooms rests on a single axis that extends throughout the house. Each space is configured differently, however, which lends the plan a sense of change and movement that is generally only achieved from a less linear organization. Some rooms rest on short sides, and some on long. Some connect through tall glass doors to covered porches, which extend their volumes even farther. They appear to advance and recede through space, though the regular rectangular floor plan never varies.

When faced with the constrained visual dynamics on the outside of such a plan, we searched for opportunities to increase the intrigue of an otherwise static footprint. We were able to bring these limitations to life through a series of vignettes, disparate moments that shift the character of the house as you move around it, or through it. At points where this brick façade steps back and hollows out, a steel frame creeps forward to capture the eye and the imagination. It appears as if the brick has gradually eroded in these places, exposing the steel like a skeleton that has lived inside the walls of the building. This narrative is contrasted by moments of inversion, where steel punches through the brick to create balconies, trellises, and railings. Together, these elements animate and embellish the design, while also providing some color and material contrast to the pale bricks that make up the rest of the house.

This long plan, in combination with the substantial tree presence and limiting terrain, results in a house that cannot be viewed satisfactorily from any great distance. Rather, focus is drawn through the body of the house or around its perimeter, to the view beyond. On a sunny day, light seeps through an alignment of windows on either side of the first floor, illuminating the interiors and lending a lightweight quality to the structure. The materials that we chose for the exterior complement the natural tones of the surrounding landscape, with masonry that replicates the look of local limestone. This allows the house to sink back into the site, all but disappearing from view.

Inside, interiors by Ashe Leandro lend the space an almost museum-like quality. Each object holds its own space within the overall composition of the home. Every piece of furniture has a curve, or a line, that draws the eye and draws movement toward it, too. Their colors complement the blues and greens that seep into every room from the nearby windows. Outside, the terraces and porches are meant to be utilized year-round, creating shade and inviting breezes in the spring and summer, with fireplaces and heaters providing a place to gather and keep warm during the colder months.

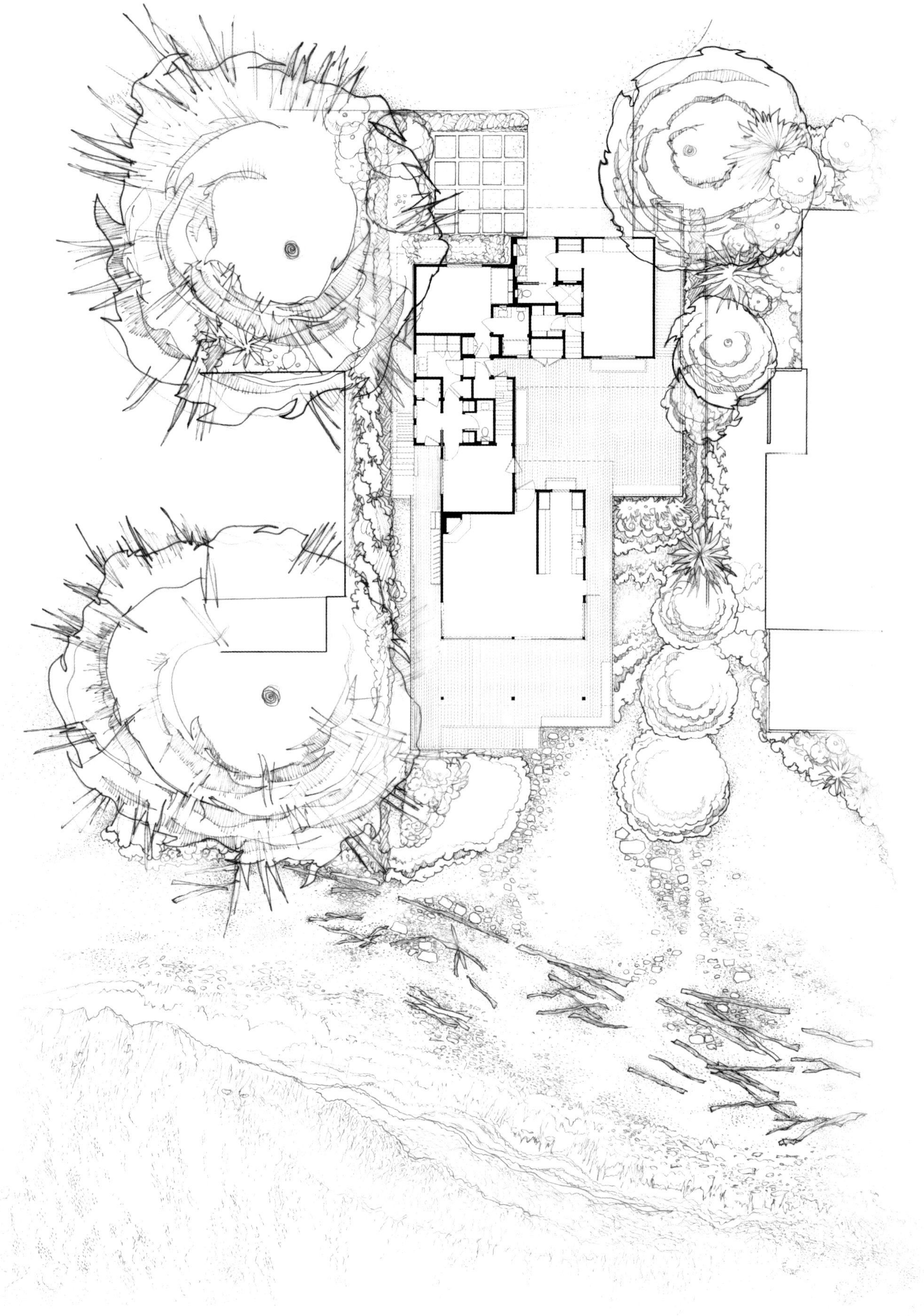

CALIFORNIA
HOUSE

0 6 12 24 FEET

XV. CALIFORNIA HOUSE

Rincon Point, a prime surf break on the coast of California, first rose to prominence in the 1950s, after a pack of soldiers returned home from their service in World War II and took off in search of a much-needed respite. Back then, to make their exploits in the cold Pacific waters temporarily bearable, the surfers kept bonfires burning on the beach at all hours. Tenacity and perseverance were the wet suits of the day. By the end of that decade, the number of surfers paddling out to the swells of Rincon Point had grown exponentially, for surfing exploded in popularity in the wake of *Gidget*, a novel released in 1957. *Gidget* was the first in a series of stories told through the lens of a teenage girl finding a home within the male-dominated surfing community of Malibu Beach, and it put that culture on the map in full force. Local beaches were swamped with burgeoning surfers, and nearby Rincon, with its reliable, enticing waves, was a part of it all. These clients had been harboring a specific dream for quite some time—a dream to live right on the ocean with access to great surf, and Rincon Point was the place to be. They found a small house, also from the 1950s, and asked us to carry it forward into the twenty-first century.

The house's exposed-beam, semitransparent design took its cues from the rapidly developing style of midcentury modern architecture, which had recently made a home in California's bright and temperate atmosphere. The original architect drew inspiration from the surrounding landscape to assemble a palette of colors and textures for the house that was well-suited to its natural context. There are no soft white sand beaches at Rincon, not for several miles. Instead, large, dark rocks line the shore. The nearby trees have evolved into sturdy, spiky creatures that can withstand the harsh coastal winds. In response, the house's exterior paint scheme is as intense and dark as deep water. Rough-sawn board-and-batten siding mimics the textures of the local trees and the massive trunks that often wash up on the shore. Glass walls that let in the brilliant ocean sunlight wrap around the furthest corners of the house, framing the widest possible view of the ocean and stopping just before the neighboring houses enter into sight.

Like many coastal homes, the house is elevated several feet above sea level, to weather the surging tides. The street approach requires climbing to the level of the porch, which wraps around the side of the house in the direction of the Pacific. Originally, the house consisted of two pavilions of slightly different elevations, connected on the interior. Their change in height allowed for every major room within to share in the magnetic view of the ocean.

Our role, sixty-odd years after the creation of the building, was to enhance its features without disrupting their self-assured, elemental coherence. This rebuild was necessary because the home had no proper systems, and no insulation, which can pose a problem even in sunny California. We also added a small second story, which doubled the house's capacity for bedrooms. Overall, the changes we made were substantial, but every modification required an unobtrusive solution that deferred back to the house's simplicity. There was no need to add embellishments, for the materials are honestly used and function well in their roles. Furthermore, we were able to preserve several of these distinct material choices from the original construction that bring a world of character to the house. The most notable of these was the liberal use of local redwood in the interior design, no longer a possibility for modern-day construction. These wide planks were left unfinished, and they have spent the last several decades developing an irreplicable and irreplaceable patina that belongs entirely to the site.

The house's overall lack of pretense has become a precious quality and commodity as time has progressed. It has maintained its clarity in a completely unselfconscious manner, and we were glad to contribute to the retention of such a characteristic place.

SURF TRIBE
James Salter

SURFING
BACK IN THE DAY
HIGH TIDE
London
THOMAS HAMEL
HORSE SOLDIERS
MIRACLES
Beautiful Beach Houses
Ellsworth Kelly

Surf Shacks
Surf Shacks

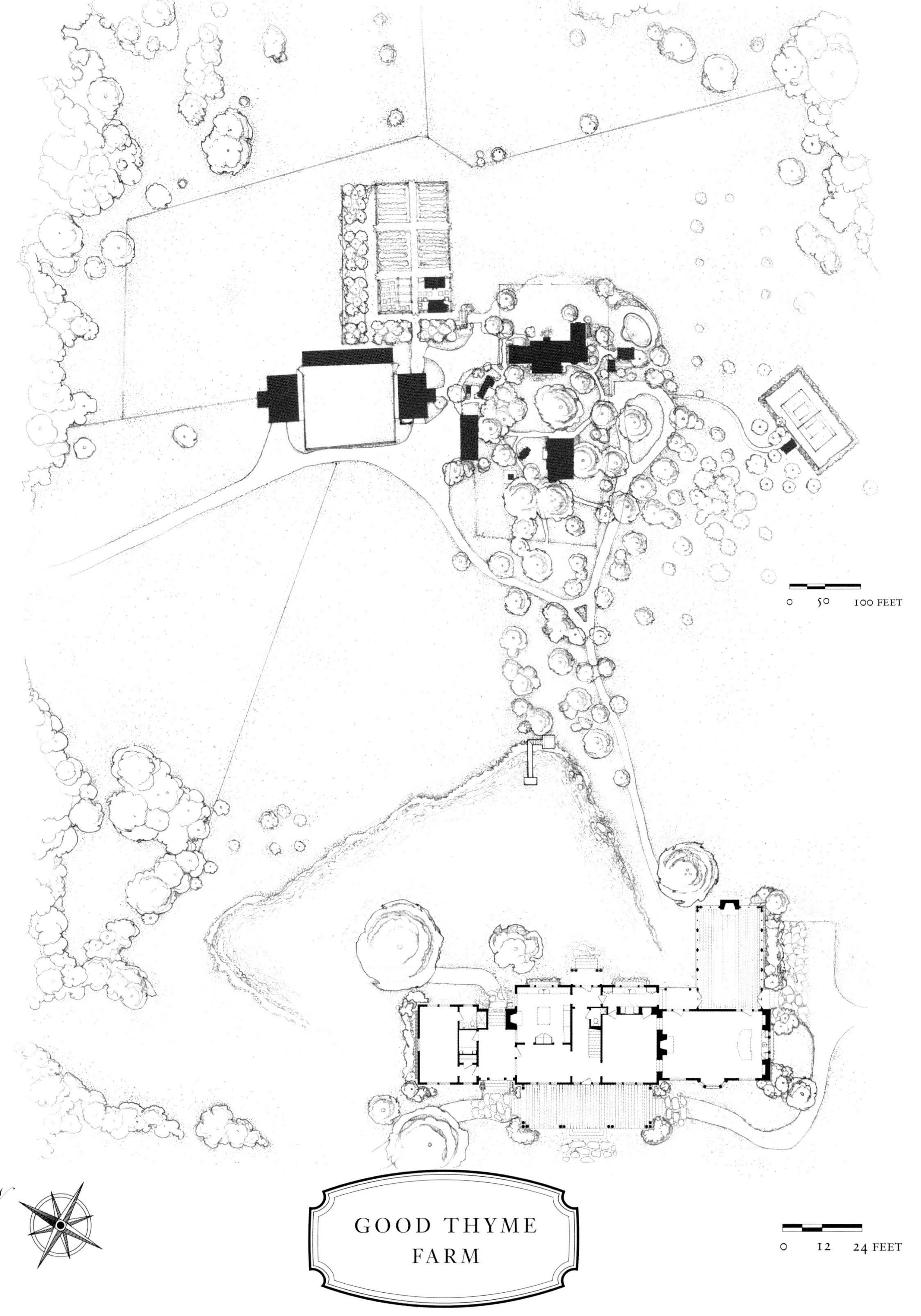
0 50 100 FEET
N
GOOD THYME
FARM
0 12 24 FEET

XVI. GOOD THYME FARM

An hour west of Houston lies Good Thyme Farm, an appropriately named and moderately sized garden operation that our restaurateur clients use to support their farm-to-table city eateries. We were approached in recent years to design a central residence for the property that could support the social needs of a family who often finds their culinary, agricultural, and personal worlds spilling over into one another. In meeting these desires, we sought to produce a visually dominant building, whose thoughtful placement would reorient the existing guest accommodations around an open lawn in the manner of an academic quad.

To generate a richer experience for a structure such as this, we deferred primarily to the story of the landscape. The new house's orientation on the property engages comfortably yet purposefully with a voluminous group of trees, carefully nestling the body of the house in and around the massing of their foliage, a placement that leaves a resonant impression of maturity and harmony within the mind of the viewer. In a matter of years, it will no longer be evident whether it was the house or the trees which came first.

Stylistically, we found that ceding to the white wooden clapboard façades of the surrounding homestead was an appropriate choice when subjecting the preexisting family compound to a new element. In the face of this material similarity, our building warranted further distinction of another kind; we referred predominantly to an interpretation of modern Greek Revival architecture to evolve the language of the design. A simple version of that visual vocabulary gave the house its desired hierarchical primacy on the quad and a sense of formality from every viewpoint: a balanced plan with two subordinate transverse wings that extend from either side of a central mass, subtly detailed Doric columns and pilasters, large double-hung windows, and dormers with scaled pediments above them. Despite their relative simplicity, this blend of classical and vernacular characteristics read as consequential due to the scrupulous nature of their rendering. In this manner, the house maintains a consciously commanding presence over the surrounding area, its recent construction notwithstanding.

The plan of the house is modest and familiar: it consists of a central stair hall with the principal living and dining rooms grounding the first floor, and bedrooms scattered around the stairs above. New York–based designers and long-term friends of the firm, Miles Redd and David Kaihoi, are responsible for the zestful, chic, and eclectic interiors found throughout. From the kitchen, the family can cater meals to feed dozens of guests at a time, and there are plenty of beds available to support guests who stay over. Various ancillary components augment the basic plan and give the appearance that they were added gradually, as the need arose. The porch that projects off the back end of the living room to provide supplemental room for hosting or relaxing is one example, a mock addition on the end of the house's symmetrical core. On the front side, a separate, formally ordered porch lends clear views of the fire pit, renovated camper van, original Victorian house, and toy-strewn lawn around which they are all now oriented.

We built elements outside this quad as well: new barns, gardens, animal pens, tennis courts, a tent pavilion, and a pool complex. The pool presented a minor problem, as its designated location on the right-hand side of the main house fell on a parcel of land that sloped down gradually toward the grazing pasture below. In keeping with the aesthetics of a country residence, we mediated this topography by using a ha-ha wall as the retaining edge of the pool's landing. A ha-ha wall, named for the element of surprise one feels upon the discovery of said trick, is a recessed element of landscape design that creates a one-sided vertical fence while maintaining an uninterrupted view of the landscape from the elevated and protected edge. Poolside, one hardly notices the dip in elevation or realizes that a fence has been created, a sure sign that the feature operates well within the preexisting flow of the landscape.

GENIE
DIRECTION DE PARIS
ATLAS DES BATIMENTS MILITAIRES

AMERICAN WEST

N
BRANARD
HOUSE
0 4 8 16 FEET

XVII. BRANARD HOUSE

It is a truth universally acknowledged that any architect who would willingly obscure the entire façade of their newly built house behind the foliage of an enormous oak tree must be married to a landscape architect. This was indeed the case with this house, the first independent construction project that a partner in our firm has carried out for the use of his own family—under the full attention of his spouse. We, the architect and client, were drawn to the site because of the greatness of the tree, which tied the property to the history and identity of the surrounding area. In this neighborhood, the Menil Foundation has gracefully cultivated a unified campus from their vast and gradually accumulated acreage through the construction of several art buildings, careful tending of landscape, and mindful emphasis on pedestrian prominence. Our tree was one of many that had long characterized the area, and we were glad to preserve it, even though it left little room for other landscape or architectural features. It was clear from the start that whatever we built on the site would immediately enter into dialogue with the tree.

In a case of a perceived constraint spurring creativity, the context for the house generated very rapidly. The large canopy and mass of sprawling branches occupied a sizable proportion of an already compact lot. Their impressive reach reinforced our desire to construct something small, something which sits lightly on the earth. We responded with an L-shaped house of an archetypal Arts and Crafts plan that could operate efficiently with a small footprint. In its simplest form, the plan consists of a central stair with two large rooms situated on either side: a library, and a combined living and dining space. Bedrooms and smaller, personal rooms occupy the second floor. We reflected a similar Arts and Crafts quality in the interior of the plan, through the employment of a simple tectonic language. One type of door is set into one type of paneling, one type of cabinetry sits below one type of ceiling, and so forth. This clarity of language allows for the playful, variable manipulation of a visual narrative that courses throughout the house, visible where the paneling of the entry hall wraps around a corner and sweeps upward to become the stairwell. The top of this transforms into the back of a cabinet on the second floor, as the handrail of that stair rises and converts into the same piece of furniture.

As the house's two wings unfurl around the tree, they work to establish a hierarchy of sufficient height and meaning to hold their ground on the site. A line of transom windows wraps around the first floor to establish two scales within the elevation; the first relates comfortably to a human register, and the second to the height of the tree. This characteristic sets up a relationship between the inside and the outside of the building and provides a moment of competition with the tree. The shingles and windows are purposefully large, to relate to this conflict of scale. The white boards that lace the windows together on the second floor bring an awareness of hierarchy to each level of the elevation.

Inside, Wolf Holden Design Studio's transformative handling of the interior design amplifies the transparent nature of the house. With greens and blues, the firm wove a complex, multilayered tapestry of materials whose tones and values function as a cohesive whole that grips the unconscious mind. Wolf and Holden love color, and green more than anything. They refer to it as a neutral, for its natural affinity to pair with any warm hue. At the start of her involvement, Wolf recalls being impressed by the story her clients provided, one that was complete and coherent, centered around a deep love of creation. "There was this sense of wanting very handmade things . . . and everything was sketched at a meeting," Wolf commented. In the powder room, hand-painted wallpaper by decorative artist Anne Harris provides a point of confluence between this tactile creativity and the clients' many other passions.

Conceptually, the exterior of the house was influenced by the neighboring community of small wooden bungalows, the expressive yet modest structure of the nearby Menil Collection, and the towering stockpile of meaningful references gathered by the architect over the several decades of his practice. No single element of the final design owed its evolution to an exclusive point of inspiration. Rather, the vernacular language of wooden houses blended with the lean and long, shingled, California-based architecture of Ernest Coxhead and William Wurster. A similar mixture of choices concerning the contrast of color and material relates to John Staub's local interpretations of Harrie T. Lindeberg's American houses. Their comfortable colors and details were another point of confluence where economical, appropriately modest, and long-standing ideals met and melded together.

ATLAS
NATIONAL GEOGRAPHIC ATLAS OF THE WORLD
TITAN
THE LAST LION
PORPHYRIOS
CLASSICISM AT HOME
ROBERT A.M. STERN ON CAMPUS
HOUSES
DESIGNS FOR LIVING
HENRY HOWARD
THE ENGLISH HOUSE
Modern Design 1890-1990
MCKIM, MEAD & WHITE
NEW YORK
NEW YORK
SCULPTURE
SCULPTURE
SCULPTURE
SIR EDWIN LUTYENS
SIR EDWIN LUTYENS
ISTANBUL
Caillebotte

Gardenista
SARGENT & SPAIN

A HISTORY OF
MODERN ART
BURNING DOWN THE HOUSE | JANE MENDELSOHN
Nothing Daunted
DOROTHY WICKENDEN

VERMEER
American Watercolor

INSIDE
TANGIER

SARGENT
TREVOR CHAMBERLAIN

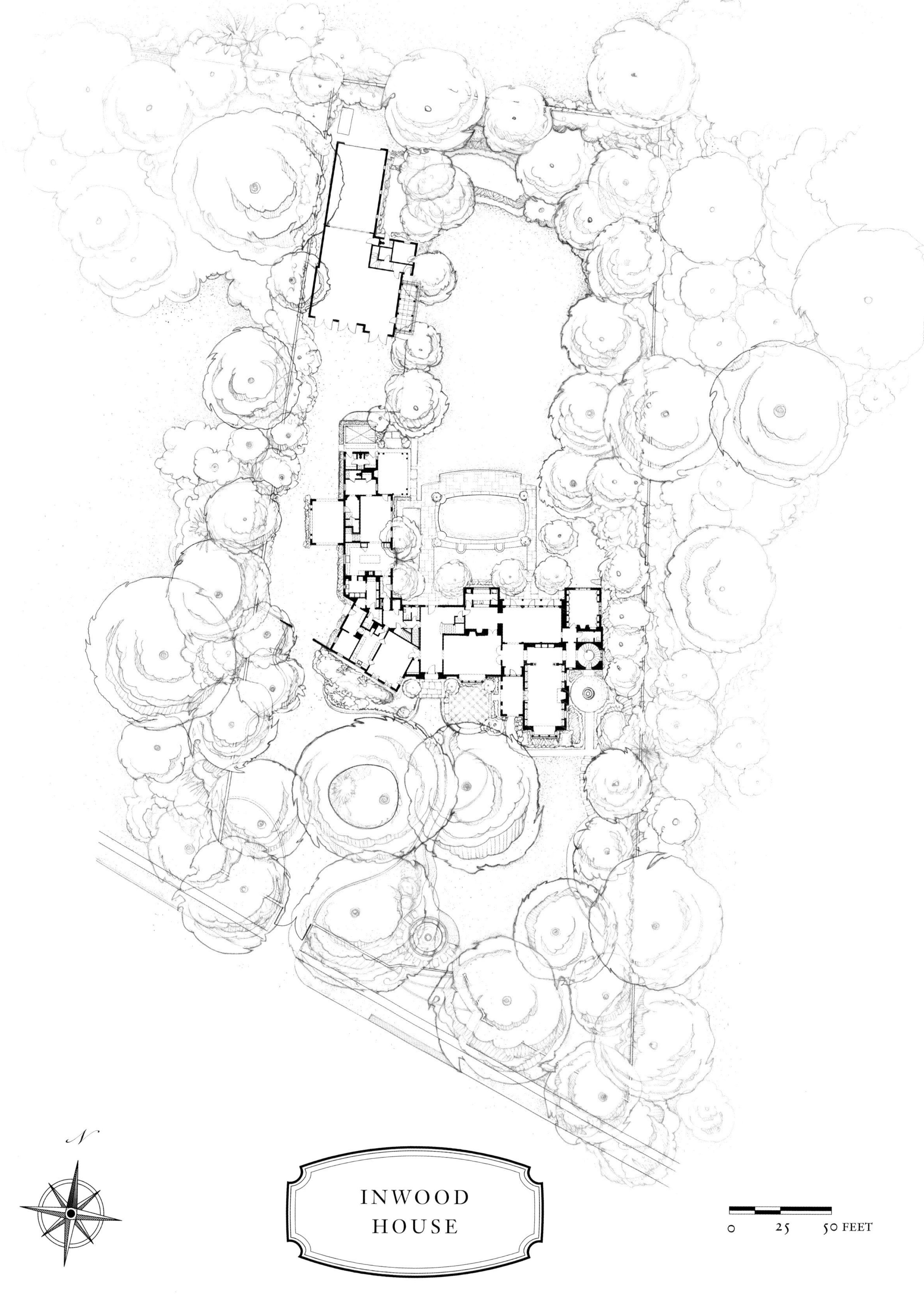
N
INWOOD
HOUSE
0
25
50 FEET

XVIII. INWOOD HOUSE

The houses of the early twentieth century are distinct from the houses of today, for they lack many of the contemporary amenities that we have come to consider as normal inclusions in most homes of a certain scale. Where they used to have libraries, we now prefer private offices; kitchens and closets have grown dramatically in size and aesthetic appeal; mudrooms, family rooms, and exercise rooms are all relatively recent developments, though they have ceased to feel uncommon. Century-old houses on estate lots in River Oaks, such as this one, have thus far withstood demolition because they had enough space to tolerate the way lifestyles have evolved through the years. As times and tastes change, older houses with sturdy, spacious tectonics can be modified to accommodate an increased desire for contemporary amenities that may not have existed when the house was built. The first owner of this late 1920s Tudor-style house had attempted to address this rising tide of needs by adding wings on either side of the main structure. Several decades later, our clients engaged us to tackle the same issue, to more comfortably accommodate even more contemporary desires.

Our clients were fond of the original house's large, formal rooms and desired to keep them intact. We were amenable to this, for the living, dining, and entry spaces had maintained their merit even when the secondary wings had not. First, we removed those previous additions. In their place, we situated two masses on either end of the house to create projecting *L* shapes. These perpendicular additions to the main core allowed us to control the revamped exterior space; the landscape architecture now supports the planning, but also becomes a participant, in dialogue with individual rooms and the overall flow of the house. For instance, we created a mahogany-paneled, Edwardian-inspired library that juts out perpendicularly from the bulk of the structure. Drawing this room away from the house not only took the library out of the flow of traffic from one room to another but allowed for three walls of French doors to open up directly onto the yard. Outside, we created a covered terrace in the corner where the exteriors of the library and living room meet, establishing a new outdoor feature that ties together both spaces while retaining its own function and identity as a sheltered, private alcove.

Not all spaces necessitated a grand architectural treatment on the interior, for we knew very early on in our process that the interior design work would be the cornerstone of this built environment. We owe the striking character of this renovation to Charlotte Moss's prodigious handling of that design. When the New York–based designer arrived on the scene, she treated our work not as a recent element to be molded, but as a preexisting canvas over which she could apply a wash of topical decor to suit every space. Moss built up each room, from the smallest teaspoon to the largest marble mantelpiece, in a manner entirely appropriate to the nature of the house and our clients. Her work is transportive; the decorative worlds that she builds inside an architectural environment address fashion and function in equal measure. From the attenuated Bonacina wicker of the garden room to the green, leather-covered walls of the bar, each space establishes a moment for itself. On the wall above the main staircase, Moss commissioned the painting of a flock of local birds, rendered at life size by decorative artist Bob Christian. By diversifying the types of frames in the gallery-hung corner, Moss soulfully amplifies an otherwise nominal space, bringing life and meaning to her clients at every turn.

Throughout this project's development, we worked with the house—not against it—consciously reassembling the core with its memory still intact. In doing so, we were able to retain the essence of the original construction, while carefully nudging it into a new era of existence. We believe that we have given this house the proper tools to face whatever challenges that future trends in architecture may bring, just as our predecessors would have done in their time.

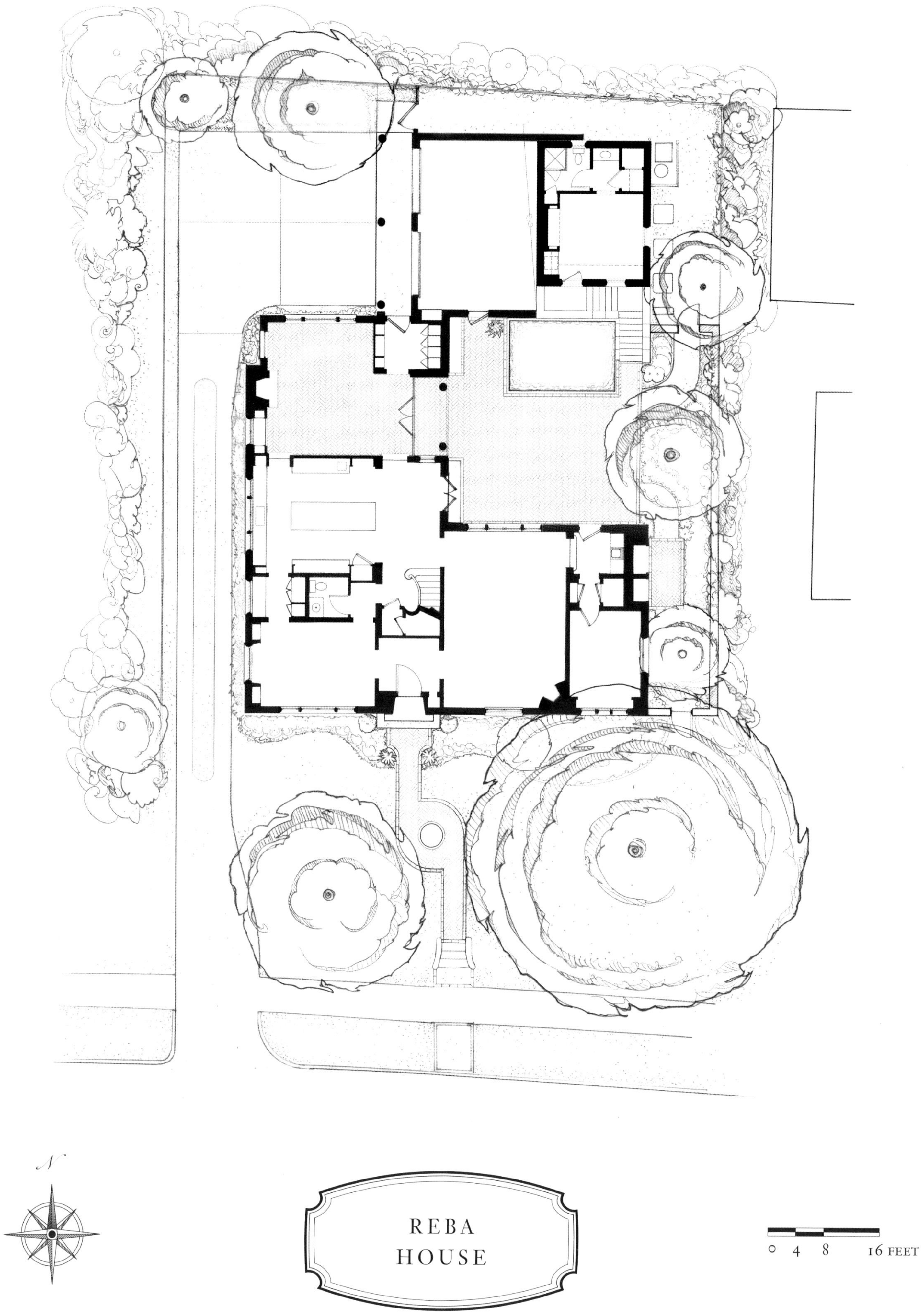

N

REBA
HOUSE

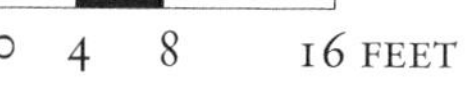
0 4 8 16 FEET

XIX. REBA HOUSE

It is a rare thing, in our experience, for a new house to feel entirely at ease within its own community, wholly capable of standing alone yet possessing no real desire to do so. The unique posture of this project is defined by the character of its street, as so many houses in the highly variable neighborhood of River Oaks are. These streets branch, curve, circle small roundabouts, straighten out, turn into broad boulevards, cross major roads, and, occasionally, envelop sizable mid-block parks. The lucky few houses that border these immured parks tend to focus interest on their façades, the size of their lots reduced to accommodate the expanse of the social green space.

We responded to our client's wishes to blend in with a typical 1920s house type, which could contribute positively to the historical language of the neighborhood without drawing undue attention to itself. The front door opens onto a shallow entry hall, with the living and dining rooms positioned on either side. Large windows enhance the perceived scale of these smaller rooms, filling them with light and opening them up to an expansive view of the park beyond.

We approached the interior architecture with intentional simplicity, allowing purity of form to eclipse visual complexity wherever possible. The clarity provided by these sculptural details is plainly visible throughout the house, such as in the living room, where the lines of a plaster fireplace recede smoothly upward to blend into a corner of the ceiling. In the nearby stairwell, a ribbonlike stair evolves upward, ascending to the light above. Mahogany millwork begins to distinguish itself from the white walls of the interior, as an undulating light fixture, draped in gauzy fabric, casts oscillating shadows across the walls of the stairwell. In the kitchen, a cheerful checkerboard tile floor contrasts pleasantly against pale blue cabinetry and an iridescent backsplash. New York–based design firm Ashe Leandro is responsible for these contrastingly contemporary interiors; their thoughtful mix of chic and crafty elements plays well off the comparatively simple walls, for the smallest fragment of detail work becomes almost ornamental in this understated environment.

Outside, an intimate courtyard acts as an extension of the family room, its presence, visible from so many rooms, elevating the space above that of a simple garden. Warm brick tiles take over where the kitchen floor leaves off, linking the indoor and outdoor together through tone and texture. At the base of the garage, an inviting plunge pool sits beneath a colorful tile-lined fountain. A short ornamental staircase wraps up and around one side of this pool, the water seamlessly transforming into a glimmering base for the studio apartment above. Ascending to this high vantage point, the house's architecture becomes all-encompassing. It feeds on itself, reflects upon itself, and constantly redirects focus back to its own shape, which has been carefully crafted to block out all undesirable views of the neighboring structures.

We employed materials like stone, stucco, tile, and copper to lend an additive textural quality to the exterior of the house. Olive green shutters and metal tent awnings bring color to the exterior at regular intervals. Overflowing window boxes heighten the dimensionality of the second story, bringing the pale walls to life. Windows and balconies display an ornamental, hierarchical program of metalwork that travels throughout the house, uniting the exterior with identical materials and design motifs.

Upstairs, the bedrooms are separated by short window-lit hallways. Natural light floods in from the courtyard and the adjacent park in equal measure, brightening the entirety of the second floor. The children's bedrooms are tinted with muted tones of blue and green, the sober palettes dramatically offset by bold tile work in each adjoining bathroom. The primary suite runs across the front of the house, to take full advantage of the park beyond, which stretches out below in an impressive illusion of bucolic freedom.

RAJASTHAN

GEORGE WASHINGTON SMITH
AN ARCHITECT'S SCRAPBOOK
ATLAS OF MID-CENTURY
MODERN HOUSES

ACKNOWLEDGMENTS

As we close out the process of writing this book, we are struck by the distance that stretches out behind us, and as we turn our heads to the future and the continuation of our practice, we cannot help but reflect on all that the past has brought us.

When we first founded our firm, we rented a single room in the office of our friend and fellow architect, Bill Stern. Two bachelors, we would often work late into the night to little outside consequence. In the early nineties, in the last few years before widespread computer usage, we created every single drawing by hand. But, we did not spend too long floundering under the uncertain weight of a new business, nor did we spend much more time alone. It was during this period that we met the two wonderful women who would change our lives. Jane Curtis and Vallette Windham have been constant sources of love, guidance, and support, for us and for our families, and we can not thank them enough for their confidence and partnership. We would also like to thank one of our earliest friends and mentors, Anchorage Fellow Stephen Fox, whose font of knowledge continues to overflow and inspire us. He is always willing to accompany us down a rabbit hole, answer a question, or ruminate on a problem, even after thirty years.

A short while into our career, we found ourselves collaborating with professionals out of state on our first large-scale, high-expectation project. We became a real firm nearly overnight, as our handcrafted approach rapidly evolved into one that could handle the demands of the ensuing opportunities in Houston and beyond. Each of these early projects brought us into contact with a wide-ranging network of individuals who have been instrumental to the success of our work, including our clients. We owe our success to our clients—their grace and assurance allowed us to become the architects we long aspired to be. Because of them, our practice has flourished. When we began to work for our very first client we felt extremely lucky, but it is only now that we can truly recognize the magnitude of that luck. Timing and circumstance gave us a chance to prove our worthiness, and we were eager not to waste it. Each client whom we have since had the privilege of knowing has extended their trust to us, and we are eternally grateful for those gestures of respect.

Our passion for this work drove us to new heights, and we found ourselves designing residential properties of considerable size in Houston, back to back, until the largest lots were no longer available. It was this passion that allowed us to feel capable of tackling projects of such an immense scale so early in our careers, and we hope that this will serve as a reminder to young practitioners in the field of architecture that it is not enough to simply do the job. If you wish to do it well, passion will carry you further than anything else.

We want to thank the enthusiastic individuals who have long shared the visions and expectations that we hold for our work, and have helped to bring them to their worthy conclusions. Every drawing of an idea is aspirational by definition. It only becomes a reality in the hands of our contractors. These fine tradespeople, the purveyors of our work, allow us to realize these ideas physically, and we commend them for their patience and diligence in doing so. If not for their efforts, our best-laid plans would forever remain two-dimensional, their idealism stuck to the page.

We have also had the great fortune to work with some of America's finest decorators, including Bunny Williams, David Easton, Mario Buatta, Charlotte Moss, Ann Wolf, Miles Redd, Laurent Bourgeois, Randy Powers, and many others. Several of these relationships have been a privileged constant since the very early days of our practice, but each new client introduces the possibility of a new collaborator, a new connection who may one day become a cherished coconspirator in the high-spirited world of design. The vision that these individuals bring to our projects reinforces and amplifies our work with great poise and fluency of form, for which we are endlessly grateful.

Beyond these external contributors, we feel privileged to have worked with many individuals within our office who shared in our growing passions over the years. To our tireless staff, a rotating cast of accomplished characters, we extend our most sincere appreciation. We have long been the conductors of an ever-changing orchestra, some members of which have had a profound impact on our practice and our lives. A few of those people have even managed to sway our opinions, which is no mean feat, as our current staff could surely attest. Many new architectural firms have grown from experience in our office, and we are grateful to have provided a platform from which colleagues could begin to tackle the professional world.

Finally, we would like to acknowledge a few individuals who have contributed meaningfully to the creation of this book.

Thank you to our friend Miles Redd, whose decorative work is joyful and inspiring. We appreciate his kind words about our practice. Thanks to Mark Alan Hewitt for his exceptional knowledge of traditional architectural practices, for getting to know us, and for placing our work in its proper context. Thanks to our merry band of photographers for bending over backwards to capture the projects within this book. We admire their talent and perceptive eyes. We thank Rogelio Carrasco for his superior draftsmanship, and for supplying this volume with such delightful site drawings. We also wish to thank our publishers, Charles Miers and Douglas Curran, for bringing this book into existence. And thank you to Lucy Curtis for listening, and for interpreting our stories so beautifully.

We are deeply indebted to the staff (past and present) of Curtis & Windham Architects. The names of those who have contributed to the work within this book are given here in alphabetical order. Significant contributions to the practice are indicated with a † symbol following the individual's name, and a * indicates the Architect of Record of Branard House.

Annatina Aaronson, Mark Anderson, Claire Andrew, Alejandro Arroyo, Samuel Baucum, Todd Beckendorff[†], Cameron Bird, James Boorman, Victoria Brenneis, Paul Brow[†], Frank Brown III[†], Charles Bullock, Rogelio Carrasco[†], Hannah Cooper, Brian Davis, Leighton Douglass, Silvia Fernandez Diaz, Michael Driskill, Robert Dudley, Spencer Esplin, Marion Evans[†], Sandy Ewen, David Farber, Leong Foong, Avery Freeman, Randall Gay, Sebastian Grande, Emily Harrion, Katherine Hart[†], Hannah Hemmer, Linda Henegar, Terrence Heroy[†], Mark Hillman, Susan Holloway, Karen Jansen, Paige Johnson, Elizabeth Kelley, Samantha Kokenge, William Lancarte[†], Catherine Love, Joel Lowery, Jane Martin, Kevin McKee, Cindy Merritt, Ruben Mijares[†], Xavier Mills, Matthew Mitchell, Megaran Morris, Jessica Most, Nathaniel Neiers, Timothy Nemec, Sarah Newbery[†], David Newman, Stephanie Nguyen, Nicholas Oddo, Mark Ofield[†], Daniel Ostendorf[†], Michael Parks, Colin Patience[†], Jenna Perstlinger, Saadia Rais, Malik Ray, Juan Reynaga-Villegas, Robert Rice, Gilman Richard, Emma Riggs, Mariana Rincon, Samuel Roberts, Greg Roffino, Mary-Bennett Sigal, Ronald Stricklin II, Patrick Suarez, Hill Swift[†*], James Taylor, Michael Taylor, Micaela Telleria[†], Heath Thibodeaux, Dudley Thiel, Theresa Thomas, Matt Vaclavik, Scott Waugh, Audrey White, Emily Wilcox, Austin Wilson, Katerina Wiltz, Chandler Young.

First published in the United States of America in 2025 by
Rizzoli International Publications, Inc.
49 West 27th Street
New York, NY 10001
www.rizzoliusa.com

Publisher: Charles Miers
Editor: Stacee Gravelle Lawrence
Design: Takaaki Matsumoto, Matsumoto Incorporated, New York
Production Manager: Colin Hough Trapp
Managing Editor: Lynn Scrabis

ISBN: 978-0-8478-7428-6
Library of Congress Control Number: 2025935211

Printed in China
2025 2026 2027 2028 / 10 9 8 7 6 5 4 3 2 1

The authorized representative in the EU for product safety and compliance is Mondadori Libri S.p.A., via Gian Battista Vico 42, Milan, Italy, 20123, www.mondadori.it

Visit us online:
Instagram: @RizzoliBooks
Facebook.com/RizzoliNewYork
Youtube.com/user/RizzoliNY

Photography credits:
Fran Brennan: 194–96; Shade Degges: 178–87; Adrian Gaut: 286–99; Paul Hester: 15, 96–109, 112–14, 121, 122, 144–55, 240–43, 253–55, 258; Max Kimbee: 18, 228–37, 260–69; Chris Luker: 2, 6, 10, 16, 17, 18, 24–37, 40–53, 56–69, 72–79, 82–93, 126–41, 158–75, 204–13, 216–18, 220–25, 272–75; Eric Piasecki: 16, 190–93, 197–201; Laura Resen: 219; Southern Living Syndication: 115–21; Trevor Tondro: 244–53, 276–83